Glory

Experiencing the
Atmosphere of Heaven

Glory

Experiencing the Atmosphere of Heaven

by

Ruth Ward Heflin

McDougal Publishing is a ministry of The McDougal Foundation, Inc., a Maryland nonprofit corporation dedicated to spreading the Gospel of the Lord Jesus Christ to as many people as possible in the shortest time possible.

PUBLISHED BY:

McDougal Publishing
P.O. Box 3595
Hagerstown, MD 21742-3595
www.mcdougal.org

Calvary Books
11352 Heflin Lane
Ashland, VA 23005

ISBN 1-884369-00-6
(Previously ISBN 1-56043-023-0)

Printed in the United States of America
For Worldwide Distribution

Preface

I remember the morning in Bethlehem in 1977 when we quite unexpectedly stumbled into "the place where His glory dwells." We had gathered to pray for a year and a half and had prayed every prayer we knew to pray. For years, the Lord had spoken to us to "sing a new song," and on this morning we just did it. Going around the room, we took our turns singing out spontaneously. When we were finished, the atmosphere was charged and changed. We did not know it, but we had just waltzed into the praise—spontaneous ones—that God inhabits. What used to be a four-hour prayer meeting that required endurance and stamina became a delightsome thing because God was in the midst of it.

When His presence comes, our hearts yearn to entertain Him—so He will stay. We found, like David, the pleasure of His heart when we sang TO Him. Formerly our songs had been ABOUT Him. His presence is the prelude to His glory. This book, *Glory: Experiencing the Atmosphere of Heaven*, serves as a gentle guide to unlocking the doors to our hearts in worship.

As I have been blessed to travel and minister from the realm of His glory in many parts of the world, I have found the most extraordinary circumstances in France and in the French-speaking countries, where the French translation has been available for over ten years. The French-speaking believers melt in worship. They are so easily touched and respond with open, longing hearts. I truly credit the availability of this book for having prepared the way. Ruth often said, "Read it three times and then put it down." When we prepare the way, God will bring the increase of His Word and truth to us.

Glory is an easy read, but the truth and revelation in the book are seeds from Heaven. As they are sowed in the hearts of people, we see change produced in lives, for we are only truly changed "from glory to glory."

May God bless you as you read and share this little book, and may all our hearts be melted to behold Him.

Deborah Kendrick

Contents

Introduction ix

PRAISE 1

As an Instrument of Harvest 3
As Celebration 33
As Warfare 45
As Ascent 73

WORSHIP 81

The Natural Progression of Praise 83
Worshiping the King — Majesty 99
Worshiping the Beloved — Intimacy 115

GLORY 139

The Glory Realm 141
The Glory Brings an Ease 157
The Glory Brings Revelation 165
The Glory Brings a Knowing 195
The Glory Brings Perspective 207

Postscript 217

Index of Songs

Praise Waiteth for Thee 4
What Glorious Days 34
Come and Let Us Sing 46
You're So Wonderful, Jesus 74
Awaken My Heart 84
I Long To See the Face of My Savior 100
I Look Upon Your Face 116
He Is So Beautiful 142
Standing in the Glory 158
Let the Glory 166
Hosanna 196
No Limitations 208
The Heavens Are Open 218
Jerusalem, a House of Prayer 224
I Ask for the Nations 226
He Gave Me 230
And So We Wait 232
So Many Miracles 235
The Flutter of Their Wings 236
Why Don't You Let Go and Let God 238
I Want to Consider You 239
Wheel Within a Wheel 240
The Glory Realm 241

Introduction

I was born in the glory one Sunday after the evening service. My parents were Pentecostal pioneers. At the time I was born, they were living in a couple of the Sunday school rooms of the church they founded in Richmond, Virginia. I was born in those rooms in the glory of God that was manifested in their ministry.

When I was a young girl, I went directly from school to the church on Wednesday afternoons. The faithful of the church were gathered in prayer from one to four. I attended most of those prayer meetings.

During the first two hours they had been making their petitions and interceding before God. During the last hour they would just bask in His presence. Those were the best times. Every petition they could think of had been made. Now the Holy Ghost took over. Sounds of glory, dropped into my spirit from those years, have kept me as I traveled all over the world in ministry.

I have been in thousands of meetings and heard thousands of sermons, but the greatest influence in my life has been those glory sounds that came forth in the latter hours of those prayer meetings where God's people touched the eternal realm.

As air is the atmosphere of the Earth, glory is the atmosphere of Heaven. It lifts us up above the earthly, into the very presence of God.

Later, when I moved to Jerusalem to live and worship on Mt. Zion, the Lord began to show me the progression from PRAISE to WORSHIP to GLORY and the relationship between the three. I have found myself sharing these simple truths with God's people all over the world. Praise ... until the spirit of worship comes. Worship ... until the glory comes. Then .... stand in the glory.

If you can capture the basic principles of praise, worship and glory — so simple that we often miss them — you can have anything else you want in God. It doesn't matter if you're alone and have nobody to agree with you in prayer. It doesn't matter at what stage you are in your spiritual development.

Move into the glory realm, and anything becomes possible!

*The earth is the L*ORD*'s, and the fulness thereof; the world, and they that dwell therein. For he hath founded it upon the seas, and established it upon the floods.*

*Who shall ascend into the hill of the L*ORD*? or who shall stand in his holy place? He that hath clean hands, and a pure heart; who hath not lifted up his soul unto vanity, nor sworn deceitfully. He shall receive the blessing from the L*ORD*, and righteousness from the God of his salvation. This is the generation of them that seek him, that seek thy face, O Jacob. Selah.*

*Lift up your heads, O ye gates; and be ye lift up, ye everlasting doors; and the King of glory shall come in. Who is this King of glory? The L*ORD *strong and mighty, the L*ORD *mighty in battle. Lift up your heads, O ye gates; even lift them up, ye everlasting doors; and the King of glory shall come in. Who is this King of glory? The L*ORD *of hosts, he is the King of glory. Selah.*

Psalm 24:1-10

Praise ... until the
spirit of
worship
comes.

Worship ... until the
glory comes.

Then ...

Stand in the glory!

Praise

Praise ... until the spirit of worship comes.

Praise — As an Instrument of Harvest

Praise Waiteth for Thee

Words and Music by Ruth Heflin

And it shall come to pass in that day, I will hear, saith the LORD, I will hear the heavens, and they shall hear the earth;
And the earth shall hear the corn, and the wine, and the oil; and they shall hear Jezreel.
And I will sow her unto me in the earth; and I will have mercy upon her that had not obtained mercy; and I will say to them which were not my people, Thou art my people; and they shall say, Thou art my God.

Hosea

Praise is a powerful instrument of harvest!

If there's anything we Pentecostal people think we know how to do, it is praise the Lord. We may be aware of other inadequacies, but when it comes to praise, somehow we feel that we already have a Ph.D. degree.

When the Lord took us to Jerusalem to live, in the fall of 1972, He spoke to us concerning the ministry to the Jews, "You don't know anything. But don't worry about not knowing anything. I'm going to teach you by My Spirit."

I don't mind the rebuke of the Lord. When people rebuke us, they leave us feeling bad. But when the Lord rebukes us, He gives us the answer to our lack. After telling us what is wrong, He says, "I will show you the way."

5

We had been in Jerusalem only a few weeks. To-gether with twenty-five young people from our camp ministry in Ashland, Virginia, we were prais-ing and worshiping the Lord on Mount Zion four nights a week at St. Peter-en-Gallicantu (a beautiful Catholic church built over the traditional site of the house of Caiphas, the high priest in the time of Christ). During the daytime we attended Hebrew classes — five hours daily.

One night a visiting American minister, who had been working in Nigeria, spoke to us. He looked over our group of young people, saw that they were all vigorous, and decided that they should be out passing out tracts. With his past experience he could visualize how we could reach the whole city of Jerusalem in a short time, and he was calculating how many thousands of tracts could be distributed. "You must be out sowing the seed," he said.

Everything the brother said was biblically true. We believed in sowing the Word and had done great Bible and Gospel distribution programs in other countries. In Nepal we even rented helicopters to lift us into remote areas with our Gospels and crossed barriers, with the help of the royal family, to distribute them. But in Jerusalem, there were cer-tain restrictions. If we were going to live there, we would have to abide by the law.

What the brother said was biblical, but it just

wasn't God's answer for Jerusalem at that time. In every country God has a plan. There is not necessarily one single answer that works everywhere or one practical solution that fits every situation.

As the brother was speaking, however, I could sense that our young people were being challenged. I could visualize twenty-five young people lined up the next morning to ask, "Where are the tracts? We are ready to go give them out."

That night I prayed, "Lord, give me Your answer for them."

In the middle of the night the Lord spoke to me. He said, "You sow to the heavens, and I will sow to the Earth." That was the way our ministry of praise on Mount Zion was born.

I didn't have a precise Scripture verse at hand to back up what God was saying to me. And I didn't understand yet all that He meant by "You sow heavenward, and I will sow earthward." But I was determined to learn.

Night after night we gathered to praise the Lord. He spoke to us and said, "You are only beginning to praise Me. I will teach you by My Spirit how to praise Me." I'm still learning.

When we had praised Him for a while, we would receive a prophetic word in which the Lord would say, "Your praise delights Me. It thrills My heart. It pleases Me. But I want you to praise Me more." We quickly learned that praise so delights the Lord that He always wants more.

There is a teaching going around that "praise is for the immature, but intercession is for those who are spiritual." That couldn't be further from the truth. In Revelation, one of the great praise books of the Bible — in reality, the praise and worship book of Heaven — we read:

> *And a voice came out of the throne, saying, Praise our God, all ye his servants, and ye that fear him, both small and great.*
> *And I heard as it were the voice of a great multitude, and as the voice of many waters, and as the voice of mighty thunderings, saying, Alleluia: for the Lord God omnipotent reigneth.*
> Revelation 19:5-6

Who are these *"servants"* who are called to praise as late in God's calendar as the nineteenth chapter of Revelation? They are *"all"* His servants. If praise were immature, then we certainly would outgrow it before eternity.

The people whom He calls to praise in this passage are described further as *"ye that fear him,"* and finally as *"both small and great."* All of us must praise the Lord. This is one realm in which we are all equal.

He calls both the *"small"* and the *"great"* to praise. We are all one in the realm of praise.

In response to God's call, John described what he heard as *"the voice of a great multitude."* The greatest instrument of praise that God has given us is the voice. Learn to lift it up to God.

We discovered not only that praise delighted our God and He desired more of it, but also that He liked it to be louder. Not only does He urge us *"praise the Lord."* He tells us to praise with *"the voice of thanksgiving"* (Psalm 26:7), *"with the voice of triumph"* (Psalm 47:1), *"with the ... voice of a psalm"* (Psalm 98:5), and with *"the voice of rejoicing"* (Psalm 118:15).

The voice John heard was *"the voice of a great multitude,"* *"as the voice of many waters,"* and *"as the voice of mighty thunderings."* Our praise rises until it thunders like Niagara or Livingstone Falls, so great are the rushing sounds of the joining together of voice to voice. It rises further until it is *"as ... mighty thunderings."*

The voices that John heard were saying, *"Alleluia: for the Lord God omnipotent reigneth."* A voice of praise is always a voice of victory. That is why the enemy fights praise. You can't praise very long without entering into victory. You can sometimes pray about a matter, and the more you declare the problem and pray around it, the more your faith begins to wa-

ver. You see the problem first as it is. Then, it becomes even bigger than it really is. And finally, it
becomes overwhelming. But when you praise, you
always enter into victory. Praise is entering in. *"Enter into his gates with thanksgiving, and into his courts
with praise ..."* (Psalm 100:4).

Praise is not the end. It is the beginning. It is the
entering in. Many Pentecostal and Charismatic
people have learned to enter in through praise, but
they have not known how to continue on into worship, and further into the glory. Praise is just the
entering into His presence. We enter in through
gates of praise.

When New Year's Eve came, we had been praising on Mount Zion for about six weeks, constantly
urged on by the Lord to more and deeper praise.
We were not only praising Him with our lips, we
were praising Him with the clapping and the up-
lifting of our hands and with dancing, all wonderful
and biblical forms of praise.

On New Year's Eve the Lord spoke to us: "Even
now, while you are praising Me, I am pouring out
My Spirit in another part of the city." We got so excited. We could hardly wait until the next day to
see what God had done in some other part of the
city.

The next day we learned that a group of twenty-
five Arab Baptist young people had gathered for a

social evening when suddenly the Holy Spirit had been poured out upon them and they began to speak in other tongues. Twenty-five at that time in Jerusalem was like two thousand five hundred in the United States.

How thrilled we were! We were learning, as Micah the prophet said, to know God's ways.

> *And many nations shall come, and say, Come, and let us go up to the mountain of the LORD, and to the house of the God of Jacob; and he will teach us of his ways, and we will walk in his paths: for the law shall go forth of Zion, and the word of the LORD from Jerusalem.*
>
> Micah 4:2

God had promised to teach us, and He was doing it. The Church has tried too long to do God's work with Madison Avenue methods. We've tried to do God's work with the methods of man. We've tried to do God's work with our own understanding. But when we do God's work in God's way, we get God's results.

We had so much to learn. We were not nearly as bold and liberated as we are now. God has been working on us for a while. But once you find that something works, you want to try it again. We began coming to the services with greater anticipation and praising the Lord with greater fervor. Several weeks later, the Lord spoke one night and said, "While you are praising Me, I am pouring out My Spirit in Gaza." We began to hear reports of the outpouring of the Holy Ghost in Gaza.

A few weeks passed. God spoke to us of an outpouring of His Spirit in the Galilee. Subsequently we heard of the outpouring of the Spirit in the Galilee. A little more time passed, and the Lord spoke to us and said, "I will come to My people, the Jews, and will reveal Myself to them where they are — in the *kibbutzim*, in the fields, in the factories." Jewish people began coming to our place of worship, telling us that they had received a personal revelation of Jesus.

We learned that we could praise the Lord in Jerusalem, sowing to the heavens, and that God would take our praise and sow it back on the Earth — in Jerusalem, Gaza, and Galilee — all over Israel. Later, we were enlarged to see that praise would likewise reap a harvest in the ends of the Earth. Praise is one of the most powerful tools of harvest in the Kingdom of God.

Some years ago, bumper stickers appeared everywhere bearing the slogan "Praise the Lord anyhow!" The meaning was "Praise God whether you feel like it or not. If you come dragging in from work and you've had a miserable day, just pick yourself up and start praising God anyhow." When I heard anybody say that, it disturbed my spirit.

I asked the Lord why that concept troubled me so much. He showed me in the Old Testament that when any sacrifice was offered to God it had to be perfect, without blemish. We were being taught that we could offer any old praise to God and it would be accepted.

I said, "But, Lord, it's true. There are times when we come to the house of God that we don't feel well. We don't always feel like praising You. There is an element of truth to this teaching. Show me the answer to it."

We all learned a verse concerning the sacrifice of praise:

> *By him therefore let us offer the sacrifice of praise to God continually, that is, the fruit of our lips giving thanks to his name.*
>
> Hebrews 13:15

It certainly does speak of *"the sacrifice of praise."* But when many use this verse, they do so with an understanding of the word *"sacrifice"* that never existed in Old Testament thinking. The Jews had many faults, but they never complained about what they had to offer to God. "Sacrifice" to us has become that which is difficult to do, that which we seemingly have to pay a price for. So, people say, "Let's offer the 'sacrifice' of praise" — meaning, "whether we feel like it or not."

One day I was reading Isaiah:

> *I create the fruit of the lips.*   Isaiah 57:19

It suddenly dawned on me that if we are to offer the *"sacrifice,"* and the sacrifice is *"the fruit of [our] lips,"* and if God creates it, it shouldn't take a great effort on our part. When we come into the house of the Lord, we can say, "Lord, create praise within me." Then suddenly we begin to feel a little bubbling up from the innermost part of our being, and we find a "hallelujah," an "amen," a "praise the Lord," or some other word of praise coming forth. We find ourselves praising in ways that we have never praised before.

Once I saw a lady standing before the Lord with a little piece of paper in her hand. She would look at it occasionally as she worshiped. "What is that you have?" I asked her.

"This is my praise vocabulary," she answered. I didn't mind that. I knew that she was very sincere. She wanted to offer God beautiful praises. But stop worrying about a "praise vocabulary." A created praise that comes from the innermost being, even if it is only an "amen," is greater than a magnificent one that comes only from the lips. At one point I found myself repeating, "Amen! Amen! Amen! Amen!" The Holy Ghost was teaching me that He is the Amen in my life, the Final Word, the So Be It, the One who brings it to pass, the One who causes it to come into being. I didn't read it from a book, but the Holy Ghost began to birth it in me.

If you never say anything more than "hallelujah," but that "hallelujah" is a created "hallelujah," it's enough. I always tell people that the "hallelujah" I just said is not a "hallelujah" I learned when I was a little girl. Nor is it a "hallelujah" I offered to God last week in Jerusalem. This "hallelujah" is brand-new. It is just as supernatural as opening my mouth and beginning to speak in tongues. It is created.

Each one of those "hallelujahs" has a depth of meaning. When you say "I love you" to your spouse, those three words have a certain basic meaning, but they also have a fuller revelation. One time you are saying them in one context, the next time in another. The words are not static. They are fluid. They have life within them. And it's the life of the words that brings forth.

That's what happens when I am praising. That "hallelujah" is not static. It is a "hallelujah" that flows with life, with praise unto the living Lord.

I've been speaking in tongues since I was nine years old. I don't understand a thing I say in tongues, not a single phrase. On occasion, God has given me names of people or places in tongues. I remember those. Otherwise, I don't remember anything else. Speaking in tongues doesn't come through the mind. It comes through the spirit. So does the created praise that I speak.

I am not thinking, "I want to praise the Lord." I come into His presence, I open my spirit to Him, and my mouth automatically begins to proclaim His praises as the Spirit of God begins to move through me. I find myself praising God, and through the ministry of praise, I come to know Him in ways that I never knew Him before.

This is what God means by offering *"the sacrifice of praise."* It is not a grievous sacrifice. This sacrifice is pleasing and acceptable to the Lord and also to me. I find myself in the presence of the Lord, not tongue-tied, but overflowing, effervescent, not able to contain myself.

The words come easily: "You're so wonderful, Jesus. How beautiful You are. How delightsome You are. Thou art fair, my Love, so very fair."

We need to read the book of Psalms and get its vocabulary within our souls, get its character in us. We need to read the Song of Songs and let God cause our tongues, as the Scripture says, to become *"the pen of a ready writer"* (Psalm 45:1), a pen that begins to write and declare forth the praises of the Lord.

God wants us to have that flow of His Spirit within us so that we don't stand there speechless.

How many times we want to hear His voice. But in the Song of Songs, the bridegroom says to the bride, "I want to see YOUR face. I want to hear YOUR voice." God has given us a voice to be lifted up in praise to Him. If we have nothing else to offer Him, we have that wonderful voice.

Once I was in an automobile accident. I have a little dimple on the chin that reminds me. My jaw hurt too much to do any talking for a couple of days. I had heard people say, "It's just the same. I can praise Him on the inside." I discovered it's not the same. Up until that time I couldn't refute them and say it was the same or it wasn't the same. But when I had that experience of not being able to praise Him aloud, I suddenly knew that it was not the same.

There is a liberty that comes from putting your praise into audible words. It releases the river of God to flow out of you as you open your mouth and begin to declare the goodness of the Lord in the land of the living, declaring the miracle of the Lord, declaring the healing of the Lord, declaring the victory of the Lord, declaring the newness of the Lord, using your voice as a trumpet, sounding forth the blessings of the Lord.

The more you declare His blessings, the more you have to declare. The more you speak about His goodness, the more you have to speak.

I will sing of the mercies of the LORD *for ever:*
with my mouth will I make known thy faith-
fulness to all generations.   Psalm 89:1

I am going to make it known. I am going to use
this voice and use it for the Kingdom of God. I am
going to use it for the glory of God, praising Him.

Blessed are they that dwell in thy house: they
will be still praising thee. Selah.   Psalm 84:4

We will not weary of praising Him. We will be
"still praising Him." I want to be found *"still prais-*
ing" the Lord. I want to be counted among the
praisers. I'm not going to be among the critics or
the murmurers.

He wants us to be as the heavenly hosts. They
praise Him. We have greater reason to praise. We
have been redeemed by the precious blood of the
Lamb. Yet they are in His presence continually and
never cease to give Him praise — day and night.

Many people find difficulty, in their young spiri-
tuality, in coming to grips with the verse that speaks
of praying continually. In the midst of our many activities, there are times that we are consciously
praising and worshiping. But once you move into
praise and worship, even while you are working,
there is an unconscious flow of praise that ascends

to God. Even while you're sleeping, there's an unconscious praise and worship. Somebody may hear you turn over in the night and speak in other tongues. It's not that you're so spiritual. There is no effort involved.

Just as involuntary as breathing, there is a realm in God of *"still praising"* Him. You know the faithfulness of the Holy Spirit that He, the Spirit within, has taken over and is praising — even in the moments when you may have been anxious. On one level you are concerned about the next situation. And when you suddenly come to yourself, you find that while you have been on this level, pondering and anxious, wondering what the answer to your problem is, on another level the Holy Ghost has been singing a song through you. You have been singing the whole time and didn't even know you were singing.

When you suddenly hear yourself singing, you realize that the Holy Ghost was praising, the Holy Ghost was confident, the Holy Ghost was not worried. The Holy Ghost within you was at peace. That praising dimension in God was totally in control. You just needed to let that natural side go and let the Spirit come forth in ascendancy.

> *I have set watchmen upon thy walls, O Jerusalem, which shall never hold their peace day nor*

> *night: ye that make mention of the* LORD, *keep*
> *not silence.*   Isaiah 62:6

I like that. Do you see the contrast in that verse? On one side there is an intensity: *"keep not silence."* Stick with it. Do it all the time. On the other side, there is such an ease: *"ye that make mention of the* LORD."

We hear the expression "We need to bombard Heaven." God says, *"Ye that make mention of the* LORD, *keep not silence."* There is such a gentle lightness about it. It is that song of the Lord, that praise of the Lord, not hard work in prayer.

We make prayer so heavy that we all need to be spiritual "Charles Atlases" or "Supermen." That's not necessary. Just make mention of the Lord. Say, "Jesus, You're so wonderful. Blessed be the name of the Lord." Just keep on singing. Keep on praising.

In the night season you can wake up and, instead of being distressed and disturbed, you can sing.

> *And give him no rest, till he establish, and till*
> *he make Jerusalem a praise in the earth.*
>   Isaiah 62:7

God has chosen Jerusalem, and He desires nothing greater for the Holy City than that she be a praise and that she be a praise in all the Earth. That's what God desires of you and me. Sometimes our own aspirations are many. But if we'll enter in simply to being a pillar of praise, a tower of praise, a praise in the midst of the Earth, a praise in the midst of the people, God will raise us up.

Sometime after we had begun to sow to the heavens in Jerusalem, someone pointed out to us the truth in Hosea 2:21-23:

> *And it shall come to pass in that day, I will hear, saith the* LORD, *I will hear the heavens, and they shall hear the earth;*
> *And the earth shall hear the corn, and the wine, and the oil; and they shall hear Jezreel.*
> *And I will sow her unto me in the earth; and I will have mercy upon her that had not obtained mercy; and I will say to them which were not my people, Thou art my people; and they shall say, Thou art my God.*

This word *"Jezreel"* means "God sows." The Lord, who sits in the heavens, hears that which we sow to the heavens. He said, *"I will hear the heavens and the heavens will hear the earth."* In response, because we have sowed heavenward, God sows in the earth. He is not only the Harvester. He is also the Sower. We have never had a problem recognizing God as the Harvester. He is the Chief Harvester of the field. We know that. What we don't know is that He is also the Chief Sower. We thought we had done all the sowing. No! He's the Chief Sower. When I stand and begin to praise Him, I am sowing heavenward. In return, the Earth is receiving *"the corn, and the wine, and the oil,"* symbols of revival.

Some find it difficult to believe that they can stand in their houses praising God and, in this way, help to bring revival to their communities. You may affect more than your community by sowing praise. You can stand in one place and minister to the Lord and project revival to the ends of the Earth. Sow to the heavens.

If we're not careful, the things we learn as young people in God we later learn "better." At least we think we learn them "better." We leave them for some seemingly "deeper" truth. Then, God has to stir us up and remind us that He still wants the simplicity that He has already taught us.

Several years ago I was on my way to Australia. I took a special fare on a Cathay Pacific flight out of London that would pass Hong Kong. Cathay Pacific had been flying for years into Sydney and Melbourne. On my way to London, however, I saw a Cathay Pacific flight schedule in the seat pocket and was surprised to find that they were now flying from

Hong Kong to Perth. Flying directly into Perth would save me four or five hundred dollars. But would they be willing to rewrite my ticket? Usually the airlines are reluctant to rewrite tickets purchased at discount prices.

Sister Alice Ford was waiting for me at the airport in Hong Kong. "How much time do you have?" she asked.

"Well, if I'm flying on to Sydney, I have four or five hours. But if I'm flying to Perth, then I can spend the night. Wait a minute and let me see what's possible."

When I checked with the agent, she said, "Yes, we'll be glad to change it so you can fly into Perth."

No one in Perth knew I was coming, but when I got there, Rev. Don Rogers was very pleased and asked me, "Would you teach for us on praise, worship and glory for three nights?" I was happy to do that.

I taught there much as I am doing now, recounting the experiences we had in Jerusalem. After a day or two, the pastor said to me, "Sister Ruth, what we have learned is this: The way we were doing it three years ago, when we started this church, was the correct way. We were doing it that way because the Holy Spirit was leading us. Then, in the past two years we've learned 'better.' God sent you here to let us know that the simplicity in which we started was the way of the Spirit. All we needed in order to get back into the flow of the Spirit was to do it as God had taught us in the beginning."

You will NEVER progress in God so much that you discard praise. NEVER! When you hear anyone saying, "Praise is shallow," know that that person needs a deeper revelation of praise.

The Lord leads us on into greater realms, greater capacities, greater abilities, greater skills. He teaches us how to yield our members more. He teaches us how to move out more in faith in praise, how to have our faith operative in the area of praise. (Just as we have our faith operating when we pray for the sick or we minister to someone's need, we step out into new areas of praise in God.) But we will continue praising Him throughout the endless ages of eternity. We never outgrow praise. Praise is eternal just as God is and we are.

We can praise Him *"in the understanding,"* in the English language or the French or the Spanish. At campmeetings in Virginia, sometimes we have nearly thirty various languages represented. In Jerusalem we have people from about a hundred nations who come annually to praise and worship with us. How wonderful when we can all praise God together in our native tongues. Then, we praise Him in all the beautiful languages which the Spirit brings forth.

Daniel foresaw that languages would serve God

(Daniel 7:14). They serve Him as we speak words of praise, worship and adoration.

Some people have a problem with praising God in the dance. I understand that. I was one of those who believed that dancing was biblical, but was very happy for everybody else to do it for me. In those days, only a few people danced in our church — my mother and two or three others. Dancing was not as widespread nor as acceptable as it is now. I always made myself unavailable when the spirit of rejoicing was among us.

One of the bad things one learns in church work is how to keep busy with "holy activities," "holy busyness." I was at the piano or at the organ. I was always unavailable to dance. Then, one day the Lord spoke to me concerning the time that David returned to Jerusalem dancing before the Lord. When he came back into the city, bringing the Ark of God, he danced along the entire route.

> *And it was told king David, saying, The LORD hath blessed the house of Obed-edom, and all that pertaineth unto him, because of the ark of God. So David went and brought up the ark of God from the house of Obed-edom into the city of David with gladness.*
> *And it was so, that when they that bare the ark of the LORD had gone six paces, he sacrificed oxen and fatlings.*

> *And David danced before the LORD with all his might; and David was girded with a linen ephod.*
>
> *So David and all the house of Israel brought up the ark of the LORD with shouting, and with the sound of the trumpet.*
>
> *And as the ark of the LORD came into the city of David, Michal Saul's daughter looked through a window, and saw king David leaping and dancing before the LORD; and she despised him in her heart.*   2 Samuel 6:12-16

The Lord showed me that if we wanted to bring in the Ark of God, we would have to dance too.

After David had successfully returned the Ark to its place, he rewarded all the men and women who had helped him with a piece of meat, a loaf of bread, and a flagon of wine (2 Samuel 6:19). He thus became the only one in the Scripture ever to feed a nation.

Jesus fed the four thousand on one occasion and the five thousand on another. Other miraculous experiences are related in the Scriptures in which others were fed. Nobody except David, however, ever fed a nation. He did it after he came back to Jerusalem dancing. Nobody else fed a triple portion except David.

The Lord said to me, "If you want to feed a nation, and if you want to feed a triple portion, you must dance." He didn't tell me I had to dance in order to be saved. He didn't say I had to dance in order to go to Heaven. He didn't say I had to dance to be part of what is happening in the local church. He was letting me know that dancing brings an anointing that feeds nations the outpouring of the Holy Ghost. If I wanted to feed the nations a triple portion, I had to begin to dance.

I had already been to the nations. I had served the Lord in Hong Kong for four years, and had preached in Japan, Taiwan and India. In India I had preached to multitudes. I was already blessed. I had witnessed revival wherever I had gone. Now, God was speaking to me concerning a further dimension of ministry, an enlarged place in which to stand in God.

I love the challenges of the Lord! We must live by the challenges of the Holy Ghost. Something in our human nature causes us to rebel when other people give us a good suggestion. But when the Lord speaks to us, we had better listen. We also need to learn to be just as responsive to the servants of the Lord as we are to God. The servant of God is the voice of God to us in many instances.

This was a hard word for me. In fact, I had a greater struggle with this than when the Lord called me to the Chinese people at the age of fifteen. Leaving home and family to go to Hong Kong when I was eighteen was easy in comparison to what God was now asking me to do.

The Lord kept dangling that spiritual plum before me: "If you want to feed a nation, you must dance." He spoke that to me toward the beginning of camp-meeting that year. I made up my mind that every day during that meeting I was going to dance. Campmeeting lasted about a month then. Now it continues for eight and a half weeks. The first day I was so self-conscious, so sure that everybody was watching me, that everybody could see me. At our campmeeting, everyone is so caught up in the Spirit that they hardly know what others are doing. When the power of God comes, when the anointing falls, you may think that every eye is on you. But you can get lost in the crowd easily, even if there isn't a crowd. There is a crowd of angels, and many things are happening round about you.

That first day I don't think I did much more than wiggle my toes inside my shoes. I understand the problems others have in this area. I often say when teaching people, "If you do nothing more than shift your weight from one foot to the other, that's a start." But every day I made myself available to dance before the Lord. Daily I became more and more free. At the end of the month the Lord spoke to me prophetically through my mother. She didn't know what God was saying to me. Nobody had even noticed that I was trying to dance a little. The Lord said to me, "I am going to change your ministry. I am going to send you to kings, queens, potentates, people of position, and you will speak to them of Me."

I believe that dancing brings an anointing for the nations. I never let a day go by without dancing. I have danced in the rest rooms of 707's, 747's and DC-10's. How do I do it? Straight up and down.

You need that anointing to flow through you every day. Dancing brings that anointing. If you are ministering in some place where you don't have that liberty, get in your closet and dance a little before the Lord. If you have that dance in your feet, you will have an anointing to feed the bread, the meat, and the wine unto nations.

During that same prophetic word, Mother saw in vision the word *Katmandu*. Not long after that, the Lord sent me to Katmandu, Nepal, to speak to the royal family about Jesus. (That story and others like it are for another writing.) The Lord said He would send us to feed nations, and He has been faithful to that promise; but it has come through an anointing to dance. Praising in the dance is powerful!

There are certain Middle Eastern concepts that are foreign to us, but they can help us to understand God. How was it that Salome was able to get the head of John the Baptist? Her dance pleased the king so that he was ready to give her anything. Coaxed by her mother, she asked for John's head. In this case the dance was used in a negative sense.

In a positive sense, when our dance and our praise please the King, we can have whatever we want. Praise creates an atmosphere in which miracles happen.

When I dance, I always feel the anointing on my feet, and I know the promise is that wherever the soles of our feet tread, the land is ours.

> *Every place whereon the soles of your feet shall tread shall be yours ... .* Deuteronomy 11:24

I can stand in America and yet, as the anointing comes upon me, I can dance in the Spirit around the walls of Jerusalem. I dance here by the Damascus Gate, and further down to Herod's Gate, around by St. Stephen's, and over by the Gate Beautiful, around by the Dung Gate and over to Zion Gate, then up to Jaffa Gate, over again to the New Gate, and back to the Damascus Gate. I can dance around the walls of Jerusalem with anointed feet, all the while standing and believing God for the city. In like manner I have danced on nation after nation. I have found that if you dance on nations in the realm of the Spirit, God will also give you the opportunity to dance on them physically.

I'm a patron of the Catholic Bible School in Nutbourne, Chichester, West Sussex, England. Joan and Michael Le Morvan are the founders and directors. Joan said, "Ruth, I remember the first time I heard you say that you had many times danced all over the map of England even before you ever ministered here. We thought it was the most outrageous statement we had ever heard."

Well, outrageous or not, I did it. I didn't literally put a map down and dance on it, but I knew the shape of England. Many times I danced along the North Sea, danced from Scotland on down to Portsmouth, crisscrossed the British Isles, and went to Ireland and Wales. I did this by the burden and vision of the Lord.

Is it powerful? It's powerful. You can stand in your hometown and possess nations. Dancing is one of the most effective ways to do it. God will give you all the land on which you tread for Him. Our feet are anointed to possess. Many churches have Jericho marches, where you dance around the outer aisles of the church, believing God for the church, the city, the state, the nation. Well, this is just a Jericho march in the Spirit when the city is not visibly there.

At times, God has caught me up in the Spirit and I have danced around the White House, up one side of the street and down the other, and back and forth.

You can do it too: you see the White House in the Spirit and you begin to dance around it. Go down Pennsylvania Avenue and Sixteenth Street and back around by the Mall. You will, in this manner, reap blessings and victories for your nation.

Likewise, I have danced around Buckingham Palace, No. 10 Downing Street and the Houses of Parliament in London. I have danced in Red Square, around the Kremlin (for revival in Russia, etc.), and around both Germanies (for their reunification). As I did so, I remembered the vision my dear friend Debbie Kendrick had received eight or nine years before concerning the reunification of Germany and the word of prophecy she had given concerning the same. That which seemed impossible has become reality. I have danced around the state houses and seats of government of nation after nation. Rarely a day goes by that I don't dance on all the major continents.

There is power in the dance. There's an anointing for the nations. You'll find that you have an anointing to feed nations as you begin to dance more before the Lord. Don't let a day go by that you don't dance. Praise the Lord in the dance. Let that anointing go from the top of your head to the soles of your feet. Praise the Lord in the dance!

Praise is a powerful instrument of harvest!

Praise — As Celebration

What Glorious Days

Words and Music by Ruth Heflin

Therefore the redeemed of the LORD *shall return, and come with singing unto Zion; and everlasting joy shall be upon their head: they shall obtain gladness and joy; and sorrow and mourning shall flee away.*

Isaiah

The Lord had to change a lot of my thinking. We all believe we have just the correct thinking. But God is working in all of us to change our thinking. We have so many misconceptions. God is working to erase them.

I started dancing in Virginia. We didn't actually go to live in Jerusalem until 1972. I remember a girl saying to me concerning dancing, "Sometimes, when we dance in our church, we reach over and take somebody by the hand and dance with them."

I thought, "Oh, what heresy! Imagine, reaching over and ..."

We were dancing before the Lord individually. God had liberated us a little, but still I would never have reached over and taken anybody by the hand

and danced together with them before the Lord. It would have seemed too "natural" for me.

After ministering prophetically to Emperor Haile Selassie, I flew up from Ethiopia to Jerusalem for a couple of weeks en route to Bhutan to be the guest of the king there. I noticed an advertisement for a twenty-day *ulpan*, a Hebrew language course, during the Jewish high holy days — which include, *Rosh Hashana*, New Year; *Yom Kippur*, the Day of Atonement; *Succot*, the Feast of Tabernacles; and *Simchat Torah*, the Day of the Rejoicing in the Law. I enrolled at Ulpan Akiva in Netanya where Shulamit Katznelson is the director.

I didn't learn much Hebrew in twenty days. But it was an introduction to Israel. On Friday evenings we all had dinner together. It was called *Oneg Shabbat*, which means "the pleasure of the Sabbath." The Jewish people welcome the Sabbath like they would welcome a guest or welcome a queen. With the welcoming of the Sabbath came dancing and singing and rejoicing.

After we had eaten the soup, there were Hebrew songs around the table. The people sang so exuberantly. I kept asking, "What does that mean? What are they saying?" I imagined it might be a popular song, the latest on the hit parade. I discovered that they were singing songs like *"Therefore with joy shall we draw water from the well of salvation," "Israel, de-*

pend upon your God," "Rejoice with Jerusalem, all ye that love her. Be glad for her," and *"I have set watchmen upon thy walls, O Jerusalem, which shall not hold their peace day or night."* Between each course of food, more songs were sung.

At one point, each person put his or her arm around the person next to him and sang, *"Behold, how good and how pleasant it is for brethren to dwell together in unity."* Everyone swayed back and forth together.

At the end of the meal, after we had been served dessert and coffee (European style), everyone got up to dance. Again I imagined that they might be dancing to some popular song, No. 10 on the list of popular hits. But they were singing the Scriptures. And they were dancing to the Scriptures. They were also joining hands as they danced.

I was so pleased that I had gotten liberty in dancing before going to Israel. Now, all I had to do was get over the hurdle of holding hands with someone and dancing before the Lord. Also, this dancing was much more spontaneous than I had been accustomed to. I overcame my hang-ups, reached out, took people by the hand, and entered into the rejoicing.

The next year we went to Jerusalem to live with our group of young people and to have services on Mount Zion four nights a week. We danced freely during those services and during our prayer meetings. We never had an Israeli dance instructor to come in and teach us any of the Jewish dances, but the Holy Spirit taught us.

We were in prayer meeting one day. I was speaking about China. China was still totally closed. God gave us a prophetic word and said He would open the door to China. We were so excited about the prophetic word that we jumped up and danced. One of the young people, without prompting, and before we realized what had happened, put his hands up like a child playing London Bridge. Somebody else put his hands up on the other side to form a door. God had said that He would open the door to China. And before we realized what had happened, we were all dancing through the open door.

We were singing some simple refrain, "The Door to China is Opening" or perhaps "Open Doors, Open Doors," as we praised the Lord together and danced through the door. How elated we were!

And, if one door is wonderful, two doors are better. Somebody else made another door. Then, suddenly, there were many doors through which we could dance.

A few weeks later was Independence Day, one of my favorite times in Israel. It comes in May. Several of the main streets are blocked off, and everybody dances in the streets. There are high platforms every block or two with a small band and very loud music. The music is all scriptural. The streets are crowded with celebrants.

We were there rejoicing with the Jewish people (both Israelis and Jews from abroad), as well as tourists, over the miracle of Israel. We were dancing the *hora* (the round dance), when one of the young people shouted, "Sister Ruth, look over there. Look at those soldiers. They're dancing our 'door' dance."

I looked and, sure enough, they were doing that same dance. We called it "the door dance" because of the way God gave it to us. But it turned out to be a traditional Jewish dance. We had never seen them do it. The Holy Ghost had taught us.

Another morning in prayer meeting the Lord gave some word on rejoicing. One of the young people put his hand out as if in the center of a circle. Quickly, others put their hands into the center of the circle to form the spokes of a wheel. Since there wasn't enough room for everybody to put his hand in as a spoke, each one put one free arm around the person next to him. We danced and rejoiced for a time together in this wonderful "wheel," as the *"wheel in the middle of a wheel"* which Ezekiel saw.

About a week later, one of our brothers who lived in Askelon came back very excited. "Sister Ruth," he said, "when I got back to Askelon, I went to the Yemenite synagogue. And guess what? They were dancing our wheel dance. I went up to them and asked, 'Does this dance have a meaning?'"

"They said, 'Yes, this is the bridal dance. It also symbolizes victory.' "

The Holy Ghost had taught us that dance. And we were dancing around and around, taught by the Spirit of the Lord.

It is not wrong to reach out, take the hand of somebody, and dance with him, just as it isn't wrong to dance alone. The essential thing is that we praise the Lord in the dance. There is a great anointing in dancing before the Lord.

I have danced before the Lord in the streets of Moscow, as well as on the Great Wall of China. I have danced before the Lord in streets all over the world. There is an anointing for the nations, an anointing to feed a triple portion.

When David went leaping and dancing before the Lord, his wife despised him. There may be some who will despise you. When we first got to Jerusalem, we were the only Christians in town who danced. Some Christians thought we were strange.

The Jews never once criticized. They have no problem with dancing. They all dance. The mayor of Jerusalem, Teddy Kollek, dances publicly before the Lord during the Feast of Tabernacles. The eighth and final day is the Day of Solemn Assembly and is called *Simchat Torah*, which, again, means "The Day of the Rejoicing in the Law." We go out to Liberty Bell Park. There, dignitaries, chief rabbis, and leading men of the city are given the honor of dancing around two or three times, carrying a Torah scroll (the Scripture on a scroll), in one of the circles. While these great men dance on the platform, the rest of us dance and have a wonderful time out in the park.

I have seen fathers put their little sons on their shoulders on nights like this and dance for hours. It is beautiful to watch. I'm glad I don't have any problem with it.

Because we stayed true to this liberty and didn't back up when criticism came, there is hardly a group in the city that doesn't dance now. Those who once criticized us get on great platforms of the world and dance before the Lord. We waited out the criticism and watched God turn things around. They're all dancing before the Lord now and praising His name.

Why is this important? Because God is a celebrating God, and we should be a celebrating people. It is only in the past few years that the word "celebration" has become part of our vocabulary in Charismatic circles. I'm glad. The God we serve is a celebrating God.

When you come to Jerusalem, you begin to be

much more conscious of this fact. God loves festivals. That's why He has given the Jewish people so many of them. Every couple of months you have another reason to rejoice before the Lord, another wonderful holiday. He has it all planned in His calendar, and what He has planned is so beautiful.

For the Christians, Jerusalem is a city of processions. On important Christian feast days (especially Christmas, Palm Sunday and Easter) thousands of believers fill the streets in processions — singing, rejoicing and carrying banners — celebrating the Lord.

> *Thou hast turned for me my mourning into*
> *dancing: thou hast put off my sackcloth, and*
> *girded me with gladness;*
> *To the end that my glory may sing praise to*
> *thee, and not be silent. O LORD my God, I will*
> *give thanks unto thee for ever.*
>
> Psalm 30:11-12

The first time I ever saw trained dancers worshiping before the Lord was at Rev. Charlotte Baker's church, King's Temple in Seattle, Washington. The girls, dressed simply, danced up and down the aisles, skillfully yet unobtrusively, as the congregation praised and worshiped the Lord audibly. I never hear the chorus "All Hail, King Jesus" without remembering the glory of that morning.

My friend Mary Jones, a lovely Episcopalian of Sydney, Australia, is director of the International Dance Fellowship.

Perhaps one of the finest examples of this type of dancing unto the Lord can be seen yearly at the Christian Celebration of the Feast of Tabernacles sponsored by the Christian Embassy in Jerusalem. The worship is choreographed and directed by Mrs. Valerie Henry and Mr. Randall Banes.

Just as there is congregational singing and choir music, so there is congregational dancing and trained dancers. Both are valid, to the glory of God.

More and more Hebraic dances and songs are coming into the Body of Christ, bringing an increase in the anointing.

If any of you have a problem with dancing, get rid of it today. Let God give you an anointing for dancing. And those of you who have danced but maybe have not given it the emphasis it should have, let God enlarge you. Determine to dance before the Lord with all your might, with all your strength every day. Praise the Lord in the dance.

Celebrate the presence of the Lord!

Praise — As Warfare

Come and Let Us Sing

Words and Music by Ruth Heflin

Come... and let us sing un-to the Lord, for
He is worthy to be praised ....
Come .... and let us sing un-to the Lord, for

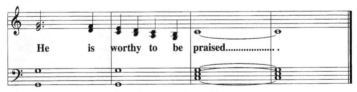

He is worthy to be praised.................. .

And when he had consulted with the people, he appointed singers unto the LORD, and that should praise the beauty of holiness, as they went out before the army, and to say, Praise the LORD; for his mercy endureth for ever.

And when they began to sing and to praise, the LORD set ambushments against the children of Ammon, Moab, and mount Seir, which were come against Judah; and they were smitten.

For the children of Ammon and Moab stood up against the inhabitants of mount Seir, utterly to slay and destroy them: and when they had made an end of the inhabitants of Seir, every one helped to destroy another.

And when Judah came toward the watch tower in the wilderness, they looked unto the multitude, and, behold, they were dead bodies fallen to the earth, and none escaped.

Chronicles

The lifting up of the hands is one of the most powerful praise ministries we have. It is just as powerful as dancing. God said:

I will therefore that men pray every where, lifting up holy hands, without wrath and doubting.
1 Timothy 2:8

When I am standing before the Lord in Jerusalem, I don't keep my hands at "half-mast." I raise them up high because I need the strength that comes from on high. Sometimes we don't need to declare any-thing. We just need to stand with our hands uplifted. That very standing in the presence of God with our arms raised is, in itself, a very powerful declaration.

When the battle was raging and Moses had his hands upraised, the battle went in favor of Israel. But when his hands began to sag, the battle went against Israel. Aaron and Hur saw it and rushed to Moses' side to hold up his hands until Israel pre-vailed.

> *And it came to pass, when Moses held up his hand, that Israel prevailed: and when he let down his hand, Amalek prevailed.*
> *But Moses' hands were heavy; and they took a stone, and put it under him, and he sat thereon; and Aaron and Hur stayed up his hands, the one on the one side, and the other on the other side; and his hands were steady until the going down of the sun.* Exodus 17:11-12

I was praying in Jerusalem when I saw a vision of Moses with his hands lifted. I saw the prevailing power manifested. Then, the Lord quickly took me to the next generation. I saw Joshua leading the Is-raelites against the Amorites. Israel had everything it needed to win the battle — except TIME. Sud-denly, faith dropped into Joshua's spirit to do something for which there was no precedent, so that there would be time to win. He commanded both the sun and the moon to stand still.

> *Then spake Joshua to the LORD in the day when the LORD delivered up the Amorites before the children of Israel, and he said in the sight of Israel, Sun, stand thou still upon Gibeon; and thou, Moon, in the valley of Ajalon.*
> *And the sun stood still, and the moon stayed, until the people had avenged themselves upon their enemies. Is not this written in the book of Jasher? So the sun stood still in the midst of heaven, and hasted not to go down about a whole day.*
> *And there was no day like that before it or after it, that the LORD hearkened unto the voice of a man: for the LORD fought for Israel.*
>
> Joshua 10:12-14

God told me that He wanted me to fly to Manila, Philippines, to stand in the intercessory position with hands uplifted for President Corazon Aquino, and that He wanted me to command time in her behalf. The week after I arrived in Manila there was a picture of her in *Time Magazine* with the caption *"Praying for Time."* God had sent her help. A week later, through the good graces of her lovely mother-in-law, Doña Aurora Aquino, I sat before the president in her office at Malacañang Palace, held her hand, and ministered prophetically to her. God has graciously granted her time. And, the Philippines is experiencing a glorious outpouring of the Holy Spirit.

All too often we have heard praise taught only from the standpoint of getting answers to our prayers. But it's much more powerful than that.

I know it works in that dimension. As children, we were never told about needs in the house or needs in the church. We knew something was happening when Mother would say, "I'm not answering the telephone today. I'm not going to answer the door today. If anybody wants to see me, I'm not available. (She was usually always available.) I'm going to praise the Lord all day." All day long she would go through the house with her hands uplifted, praising the Lord. Later, when the victory came, when the answer came, we would hear her say, "God's wrought a wonderful victory."

When she spent the day in praise, we knew there was a great need. She only resorted to that in extremity. But in extremity it always worked. Aside from extremity, praise is powerful in the advancement of the Kingdom of God.

Your praises change the atmosphere. Your praises can change the atmosphere in your house. Not all of you live in houses that have only Spirit-filled people in them, and sometimes you have to contend with atmospheres that aren't correct. If you want that atmosphere to change, just praise the Lord. Your praise permeates the room with the fragrance of God and will change the atmosphere in your household.

In the same way, your praises can change the atmosphere in the place where you work.

Do you want to change the atmosphere in your church? Stop criticizing and murmuring and complaining. Get to church early and do some praising. Stay behind a little later and do some praising. Often, those in charge are just as concerned about situations as you are, but they don't know how to change them. Praise changes the atmosphere. Go into your church and change the atmosphere by filling the church with God's praise.

Several years ago, I had just returned home to Jerusalem from ministry in Australia. In our daily prayer meeting, Maria Deans, a sister from Poona, India, had a vision. She saw a line going from Jerusalem to the middle of the Northwest Coast of Africa, continuing on to the middle of the East Coast of South America, and then proceeding up the East Coast of the United States to Virginia.

As she was giving the vision aloud, I began to follow it in vision also. I saw Sierra Leone in West Africa, Corcovado, where the beautiful statue of

Christ overlooks Rio de Janeiro, and Virginia, where campmeeting would soon be beginning.

Although I had not intended to leave Jerusalem so soon, I knew God had just mapped out an itinerary for me. I was accustomed to this — as I had traveled by vision and revelation all over the world for years before we settled in Jerusalem, and our people had done the same.

I telephoned Rev. and Mrs. Ade Jones, the pastors of Bethel Church, in Freetown, Sierra Leone, to ask them if they could use my ministry there for a week. They had been with us many times in Jerusalem. They said for me to come. I arrived in Freetown in the middle of the night to the "red-carpet treatment" — literally — the red carpet was rolled out to the airplane. Bouquets were presented. Dignitaries were there to welcome me. And the congregation was there singing songs of welcome. It was exciting.

When I called them, I made no stipulations. I only wanted to be a blessing and was willing to minister in whatever capacity they desired. I was surprised to learn they had rented the town hall. Night after night it was packed. The mayor and his wife attended, as did the president's wife and family. There was such a response to the Lord by the people. I understand that it was the first meeting where Freetown was so touched by the power of God.

I then flew from Freetown to Lagos, Nigeria, and on to Rio de Janeiro, Brazil. I checked into the hotel on the beachfront at Copacabana and went to sleep. The next day I went to the top of the mountain where I praised, worshiped and prophesied with hands up-lifted to Rio and to all of Brazil, conscious that God was changing the atmosphere over the city and over the nation. I returned to the airport, where I boarded a plane for Miami and Richmond, Virginia.

On Thursday, I called my friend John Lucas, pas-tor in Calgary, Canada. I told him what I had just done. He said he knew why I had done it. Rev. Mor-ris Cerullo was having a big evangelistic thrust in Brazil. It was billed as the fourth-largest media event in America that year. He was having a closed-cir-cuit satellite hookup to ten stadiums in Brazil and sixty or seventy auditoriums in the United States and Canada.

He initially wanted to conduct the meeting in São Paulo, because the spiritual atmosphere in that city was better than it was Rio. But, for technical rea-sons, he had to have the meeting in Rio. This was Thursday. I had been at the top of the mountain on Tuesday, and the meeting was to begin on Satur-day. God had taken care of the spiritual atmosphere over Rio.

I heard reports from a pastor's wife in the Detroit area that the power of God was so evident as she watched the crusade that she found herself prostrate on the floor by the power of the Holy Spirit. We are *"workers together with Him"* (2 Corinthians 6:1).

Your voice is a powerful instrument of warfare. You can bring the glory into any place in the world by your voice. Start praising, and in a moment you will hear the glory on your voice. It will fill the room.

We have all been in meetings that were ordinary until someone gave a prophetic word or spoke in some other anointed way. The glory came into the room by the voice and changed people's lives. There was a difference from that moment on.

> *I will bless the LORD at all times: his praise shall continually be in my mouth.*
> *My soul shall make her boast in the LORD: the humble shall hear thereof, and be glad.*
> *O magnify the LORD with me, and let us exalt his name together.* Psalm 34:1-3

Another aspect of praise that is so powerful and which we need to use more and more is singing. A number of years ago, God began to do something new in our fellowship in Jerusalem in this regard. He began to give us a new song. Now, it is happening all over the world. I am hearing messages in many circles concerning singing a new song to the Lord.

The Lord spoke to us and told us to sing a new song to Him. We didn't really know what He meant. But when God speaks to us and we don't understand, He keeps saying it until we do understand. Or He sends someone else along to say the same thing, until it begins to break forth in the midst of the people.

God is very persistent. He can have the same message for a very long time. If we are hearing the same message over and over, maybe it's because we haven't stepped into it yet. The Lord will move on quickly to something else if we catch on quickly to what He is saying to us.

He kept telling us to sing a "new song." We weren't sure if He meant sing with a different beat, sing a different melody, sing in a different style. We didn't know what He meant. None of us were particularly talented musically. One day, as we were praising, we began to sing a little song that we had never heard, never learned, never been taught, never memorized. We just sang out of our spirits spontaneously. There is more in our spirits with which to bless God and the nations than we'll ever be able to use — if we'll release it in God. We're still asking God to pour it in, "pour it in, pour it in."

He's saying, "Pour it out. Pour it out."

"Lord, I'll pour it out if I have something to pour," we say.

It's already there, but because your faith is not working in this area, you're not releasing it.

When God is leading us into something new, we are unsure of ourselves and go slowly. We put our toe in, then bring it back out, then put it in again to test the water. God blessed us when we sang spontaneously. At first we did it only in our prayer meetings in Bethlehem. When we were in the church on Mount Zion, we conducted the service as usual, as we were accustomed, with songs and choruses we already knew.

The Lord said to us, "Can't you trust Me? If you can sing spontaneously in the prayer meeting, why can't you sing spontaneously on Mount Zion?"

"But, Lord," I said, "people come ten thousand miles to be in one service. We don't want to make mistakes in front of them. What if it doesn't work?" Personally, I like an occasional stutter or stammer in a service. When we are too polished, it may be because we have done it that way too many times. We are doing it by rote, and it lacks freshness. The stammer indicates that people are moving into new territory, reaching into revelation by the Spirit.

He kept after us until we started singing spontaneously in the regular service as well. From that point on, we haven't looked back. We sing spontaneously in our services. In this way, the Holy Spirit teaches us.

How did David get this wealth of material that

we call the Book of Psalms? He sang it. He heard it for the first time when it came forth from his lips. We hear the new song for the first time when we speak it forth in a prophetic unction. It is the prophetic song of the Lord being released. David didn't sit down and think through each psalm, compose the music, and then put the words and the music together. His tongue became *"the pen of a ready writer"* as he began to praise His Lord.

And because David had versatility of experience in God, he had versatility of experience in song. Because life brought him many types of trials, he could sing about his enemies. He could sing about his joys. He could sing about his triumphs.

Outside the Greek chapel in Bethlehem, where we prayed on Friday and Saturday mornings for a number of years, we had a big sign: **PENTECOSTAL PRAYER MEETING 8 to 12 NOON**. After a while, that sign embarrassed me. I thought, "We're not really praying anymore." We were raised on travail and intercession. Now, we spent most of our time singing and dancing and rejoicing. I didn't learn until years later that many places in Scripture which speak of praying are speaking of singing. There is a singing prayer.

> *Speaking to yourselves in psalms and hymns and spiritual songs, singing and making melody in your heart to the Lord.*
>   Ephesians 5:19

There are so many ways to sing unto the Lord. There are songs of love, songs of rejoicing and thanksgiving, songs of petition, and many others.

I felt embarrassed because we weren't formally praying. Yet, it was during that time that the Lord gave me the song "I Ask for the Nations." He gave it to me spontaneously in prayer meeting, and we spent the whole morning asking for different nations. But we weren't doing it in the formal way we had known before.

God was speaking to us about the nation and showing us the answer to the problem. We were then declaring the victory, prophesying it into being, and rejoicing to see it all come to pass. We were not agonizing, weeping and supplicating as before. And we didn't quite know what to think about it.

A little later, Rev. Edward Miller, of the Argentine Revival fame, invited me to speak in what he considered to be "the greatest praise and worship churches in America," and arranged a little speaking tour for me. When you cross America, you find out what people are thinking. In every church, people asked the same questions. After about ten days I knew the one thing that was on everybody's mind: "What about intercession and travail?"

My answer to them was, "I used to be an authority on the subject. If you had asked me this a few weeks ago, I could have given you all the answers.

But God is doing something new and different. I'm not sure what He's doing."

Many times we are guilty of doing things as we have always done them, while God is moving in some new way. We're still traveling down Highway No. 1 while He's already opened I-95 to us. It's bigger, it's broader, it's faster. But we've always traveled on Highway No. 1. Highway No. 1 will get you somewhere, but I-95 doesn't have the local traffic and the impediments that slow you down on Highway No. 1. Seemingly, we would still rather stop at every red light. So, God lets us do our own thing while He has opened other ways in the heavenlies.

"I don't know what God is doing," I said to those people. "We find ourselves singing so much in our prayer meetings. Yet, we feel tremendous release in the Spirit, and we know God has heard us concerning the nations and concerning people's needs."

I went home to Virginia for campmeeting. Mother asked me to take the Sunday morning service. It was communion Sunday. God said, "Turn to Isaiah fifty-three." I read:

> *Yet it pleased the* LORD *to bruise him; he hath put him to grief: when thou shalt make his soul an offering for sin, he shall see his seed, he shall*

*prolong his days, and the pleasure of the LORD
shall prosper in his hand. He shall see of the
travail of his soul, and shall be satisfied.*

Isaiah 53:10-11

When I read that verse, I suddenly saw that not
only was salvation in the atonement and healing in
the atonement, but travail is in the atonement. And
because travail is in the atonement, I need never travail. He has done it. If I can appropriate it, I need
never travail.

When I saw it, it was so freeing. And notice this:

*Therefore will I divide him a portion with the
great, and he shall divide the spoil with the
strong; because he hath poured out his soul unto
death: and he was numbered with the transgressors; and he bare the sin of many, and made
intercession for the transgressors.* Verse 12

God the Father divides Jesus a portion with the
great. And Jesus, in turn, divides the portion with
"the strong." Who are *"the strong"*? The praisers.

When Jesus spoke of perfecting praise in the
mouths of babes and sucklings, He was quoting
from the eighth psalm:

*Out of the mouth of babes and sucklings hast
thou ordained strength because of thine en-*

emies, that thou mightest still the enemy and the avenger. Psalm 8:2

Jesus said it in a different way:

And when the chief priests and scribes saw the wonderful things that he did, and the children crying in the temple, and saying, Hosanna to the son of David; they were sore displeased, And said unto him, Hearest thou what these say? And Jesus saith unto them, Yea; have ye never read, Out of the mouth of babes and sucklings thou hast perfected praise?
Matthew 21:15-160

"Ordained strength" has become *"perfected praise."* After He has travailed, Jesus divides the spoil with the strong. Our praise causes us to enter in and possess our inheritance. We take it through praise.

"Yes, Lord," I said, "I understand now that I don't need to travail. But what do we do to appropriate it?" (There are ways to appropriate everything that God has for us.)

He said, "Keep on reading."

The chapter divisions were added to help us find our place in the Bible. We have street names and numbers to help us locate one another. These numbers only serve to help us find our location. The scroll was written and flowed on from chapter fifty-three to fifty-four. "What do I do, Lord?" I asked Him.

He said, *"Sing."*

"Sing? I can appropriate this by singing?"

"Sing," He said.

> *Sing, O barren, thou that didst not bear; break forth into singing, and cry aloud, thou that didst not travail with child: for more are the children of the desolate than the children of the married wife, saith the* LORD.   Isaiah 54:1

Notice *"sing[ing]"* and *"break[ing] forth into singing."* They are two different things. Most of you sing. Some of you are learning to break forth into singing. Singing is using the vocal cords. But there is a breaking forth into song, in which God puts a song in your spirit. You go to bed with it at night. You wake up with it in the night season. You still have it in the morning.

How many times has this happened to you? You are in a perplexing situation. You are overwhelmed. You don't know what to do, and your mind is going a thousand miles a minute trying to figure it all out. Suddenly you come to a stop sign. The car is jolted. With the jolt you focus back on the moment and discover that you're singing. You have been singing the whole time your mind's been working.

The Holy Spirit has been singing the answer in your spirit while you have been looking for the answer in your mind. "Isn't that the faithfulness of the Holy Ghost!" you say. "I have been trying to work out the answer in my mind, and all the time the Holy Ghost has been giving me the answer. Thank God for the stop sign that forced me to hear the song of the Spirit."

We're not going to sit around and prophesy to ourselves. The ministry of prophecy is for others. But song releases the voice of the Spirit within you in your language and builds you up, as praising in the Spirit does. People who prophesy to themselves have gotten into a lot of error. But I can sing. I can let that song of the Lord come forth out of the depths of my being. Some of the greatest revelations I have heard have come in song, when we have been singing and each person has been given a little verse of the song.

If we had asked, "Has anyone had a revelation this morning?" everyone would have answered, "Oh, no!" The word "revelation" is so big. It is interesting. In Catholic Charismatic circles they use the word "picture" instead of the word "vision." "Has anybody seen a 'picture' this morning?" The reason they do it is that "vision" seems so big and awesome. "No, I haven't had a 'vision.' But yes, I did see a 'picture.' No, I haven't had a 'revelation.' But I have a 'song.' "

Often, as we allow a little song to come forth, it holds such revelation. It is God perfecting praise out of the mouths of babes and sucklings. It is so beautiful, so marvelous. I keep a book each year in Jerusalem. As I sit at the piano, spontaneous phrases come to us. Beautiful vision and revelation come out of the mouths of the people. *"Sing!"*

I want you to sing from this day on more than you have ever sung before. Don't just sing the familiar choruses you already know. Let a little song come out of your own spirit. Keep it simple, one little verse at a time. Don't get too complicated.

Singing a new song does two things for you. It teaches you how to concentrate on God, and it teaches you simplicity. It is possible to be singing a chorus you know well and, at the same time, be planning a menu. You can't do that with the new song. You'll lose it. You have to concentrate on the Lord to sing the new song. Then, we need that simplicity so that we can repeat it the next time around.

> *Sing, O barren, thou that didst not bear; break forth into singing, and cry aloud, thou that didst not travail with child: for more are the children of the desolate than the children of the married wife, saith the LORD.*

> *Enlarge the place of thy tent, and let them*
> *stretch forth the curtains of thine habitations:*
> *spare not, lengthen thy cords, and strengthen*
> *thy stakes;*
> *For thou shalt break forth on the right hand and*
> *on the left; and thy seed shall inherit the Gen-*
> *tiles, and make the desolate cities to be*
> *inhabited.* Isaiah 54:1-3

God wants to bring enlargement, and He'll bring enlargement through song. Sing, and get ready for enlargement. Sing and break forth into singing and get ready to be enlarged on the right hand and on the left.

After the Lord showed me that I no longer needed to travail, someone whom I greatly respect came to visit us in Jerusalem and ministered the old teaching on travail. That teaching is not wrong. God is just showing us easier ways. I think I want to buy a typewriter because I am from the typewriter generation. But those who know how to use a computer feel that typewriters are obsolete. "What do you want a typewriter for?" they ask.

Typewriters still serve a useful purpose. But if there is a computer in the room, why buy a typewriter? Do you see what I am saying? If there is something that you can do more with, why reach back to the familiar? God is moving on. I didn't buy a typewriter.

It is the same with prayer for the sick. There are a number of formulas in the Word of God for ministering to the sick, and all of them work. I never anoint anyone with oil. I feel that God has given me a gift of healing, so that I don't come under the same category as the elders who anoint with oil. People frequently hand me bottles of oil, but I avoid using the oil as gracefully as I can. "Brother, you anoint them, and I will pray with you," I say. I am flowing in a different anointing. God has given me a revelation, and I want to flow in that revelation.

Does that mean that God is not healing through the anointing oil? No, it doesn't. God works in a variety of ways.

When I heard this person speak of travail in the traditional sense — we get down and pray until we feel in the spirit the birth pangs, feel the burden for people, as a woman giving birth, and bring forth individuals into salvation, bring forth even nations, etc. — I said to the Lord, "I really want to know if I understood You correctly. Give me a little further indication concerning this new thing."

The wife of one of our couples was expecting a baby. She didn't know what I had asked the Lord. She told me later, "That next day the Lord woke me up with this verse: *'Before Zion travailed, she brought forth.'* "

"What does that mean, Lord?" she asked.

That day she and her husband were busy, when suddenly she felt a twinge of discomfort. She mentioned it to him, and he suggested stopping by the maternity house since they were nearby.

"I know the baby isn't coming yet," she protested. "These are not labor pains."

"It won't hurt to stop," he insisted. "We're nearby."

So, they stopped. The doctor was in. He put her on the examining table and began to check her over.

"The baby is coming," he said, surprised.

"It couldn't be," she said. "I haven't done what I am supposed to do yet." (She and her husband had taken some lessons on just what to do.)

"I can't help that," the doctor said, "the baby is here."

When she told me that, I said, "Thank You, Jesus! Thank You, Jesus!"

When I hear how people are being instructed to pray, I feel sorry for them. I have one friend who gets up at five in the morning and goes through one man's formula and another man's formula and even another man's formula. By the time I got through all those formulas, I'd be worn out.

I do my best to teach the simplicity of coming into

His presence. But, even if we do it all wrong, He makes it come out all right.

At our campmeetings, sometimes we have visiting ministers who give us twenty-one steps to faith, or seven ways to be healed, or the like. My dear, saintly mother often steps forward to the microphone and says the most spiritual thing that has been spoken all evening. For instance: "It doesn't take very much faith to touch God." It's true. *"Before Zion travailed, she brought forth."* I was so excited by that.

Then I was on my way to Australia again. I was flying out of Hong Kong on Quantas Airways to Sydney. The trip was coming to a close, and toward the end of a long trip, you'll read anything. I picked up a magazine to read. It was the *Australian Woman's Weekly*. It contained new recipes, the latest fashions and a romance or two. Right in the middle of all that was this headline: **"SING YOUR WAY TO A PAIN-LESS CHILDBIRTH."** The article was written by a famous French obstetrician. He said he was not referring simply to the singing that comes from the mouth, but the singing in which the total woman is involved. When she is caught away in song, he said, she can have a childbirth without pain.

In Jerusalem, our expectant mothers use a little maternity hospital. The husband goes and stands on one side of his wife, and I go and stand on the other side. We start singing in the Spirit. We get lost singing in the Spirit, and in a few moments the baby comes. That's what God wants us to know.

If we sing, we won't have to come into that realm of travail. Why? Because the joy of the Lord brings a release of faith, and faith does the work. In a moment such as this we can release more faith for Israel and see more accomplished than in five nights of all-night prayer prayed in the realm of the understanding.

We are creating the atmosphere for miracles. Blind Bartimaeus just called out, *"Son of David, have mercy on me,"* and he was healed. When Jesus was present, things happened easily. And God will do it easily for us.

Don't let anyone else do your singing for you. If you have to start in the car, then start in the car. Most of us get enough time driving in the car by ourselves. We can't disturb anyone. Just sing. I have a friend, a Korean businessman, who calls me long-distance from Seoul when he's in business trouble. After we have greeted each other, we sing together in the Spirit. Sometimes we sing for ten or fifteen minutes.

When we are lifted up in singing, God begins to give the answers. First, He lifts us up above the cares, the problems, the needs. There is a realm of ease in God. We make spiritual things difficult. He wants to make them easy. He wants the King of Glory to come in and fight our battles for us.

Most of the time we are so busy fighting our own battles that we don't let the Lord do it for us. Remember when Jehoshaphat went out against the kings, the singers and the dancers — the praisers — went before the army. Because the praisers went before the army, they didn't even need to fight (2 Chronicles 20:21-24). And you will never need to fight your own battle if you'll move into this realm of praise and worship unto the Lord.

At one time we had a number of houses in Israel where visitors and pilgrims lived. Once we had a sister staying with us who was on a long fast. We always welcome such visitors. The problem was that she was not willing to go to church with us. I am not willing for anybody to come and fast with us who doesn't go to church. When you fast, you need the anointing you receive in the service. If you fast without going to church, you will experience difficulty.

I sent messages through all the appropriate channels, but I always got a negative response. I got more and more disturbed by her. One morning in prayer the Lord spoke to me, "Why don't you let Me handle this?"

I almost laughed. Have any of you ever laughed at God? We think we have been letting Him handle it. I thought to myself, "If the Lord can do something with her, He can do something with anybody."

"Okay, Lord," I answered. "You fight the battle." And I forgot about it. There are always another dozen problems that come up in the meantime.

When I got to church that night, who should meet me at the door but this sister who had continually refused to come. She not only met me without being coaxed, she met me with an apology. "I was praying today," she said. "God spoke to me that my spirit had been wrong and my attitudes had been incorrect. I'm sorry."

"How foolish we are," I thought. "We think we are letting God fight the battles, but we're not really." The more we sing to Him, the more He will fight the battles.

Praise is a powerful weapon of warfare!

Praise —As Ascent

You're So Wonderful, Jesus

Words and Music by Ruth Heflin

You're so wonderful, Je.........sus......, You're all my heart has

wait.......ed for............. . You're so wonderful, Je..........sus........, I

on............ly want to love You more .... You're so wonderful,

Je................sus ...., I praise and worship and adore...............

.... You're so wonderful, Je........... sus .... . My won..der.. ful.....

Lord.

Lift up your heads, O ye gates; and be ye lift up, ye everlasting doors; and the King of glory shall come in.

David

You can praise God when everything around you is totally cold, and believe God to create praise within you. When I come into the Lord's house and I begin to praise Him, I must be conscious that I'm ascending. I'm ascending the hill of God. I'm coming up into the high place of the Lord.

Have you ever ridden with somebody who was just learning to drive without an automatic transmission and was using the clutch on a hill? (Jerusalem is built on hills; and most of our cars don't have automatic transmissions.) I've ridden with some people who didn't quite have a grasp of the clutch yet. As they began to ascend a hill, they would go up a little and slide back a little, go up a little and slide back a little. The ride was very jerky. Have you ever been in a song service that was like that? You experience spiritual whiplash.

The person leading the service begins to sing, and you feel yourself ascending. Then he does something else or perhaps changes rhythms and you slip back down. With the next song you go a little higher, then slip back again. By the end of the song service, you have spiritual whiplash. This happens because the song leader hasn't learned to ascend in the Spirit.

Sometimes it's better to sing fewer songs. When the anointing falls on a particular song, stay with it until you get to the top of the hill. It's not the song that's important, it's the anointing. The anointing is like the gasoline in the car that will take you to the top of the hill.

Some song leaders insist on singing a chorus twice or three times, no matter what the Spirit of God is doing. Sing until you get to the top of the hill. Be conscious that you are ascending the mountain of the Lord. Don't stop praising till you get to the "holy place."

Sometimes it takes fifteen minutes of singing and praising. Sometimes it might take ten minutes. On another day, in another service, it might take twenty. At another time, it might take only seven. Or you may get so hungry for God that you run quickly up the hill of the Lord and get there in three. The time will vary, but there will always be the ascent. There is always the entering in. We come from the outside world. And we always *"enter into His gates with thanksgiving and into His courts with praise. Be thankful unto Him and bless His name."* Praise is the entering in, and praise is also the ascent.

Jerusalem is more than two thousand feet in altitude. Throughout the Scriptures there are references to the tribes going "up to" Jerusalem and "up to" the house of the Lord. The "house" of the Lord was built on the "hill" of the Lord, so the "hill" of the Lord became synonymous with the "house" of the Lord and the "holy place."

In Hebrew, one always uses the verb *laalot,* "to go up," in connection with Jerusalem. One does not "go up," *la-a-lot,* to any other city in the world. Even if one lives in a city that has a higher altitude than Jerusalem, one still speaks of "going up" to Jerusalem.

It is the consciousness of the Jerusalem of the earthly representing the Jerusalem of the heavenly. So, in praise, one must always be conscious of going up to the holy place.

> *Who shall ascend into the hill of the LORD? or who shall stand in his holy place?*
>
> Psalm 24:3

The late Sister Jashil Choi, Dr. Cho's mother-in-law, was my good friend. We conducted conferences together in Jerusalem. She called me sometimes from

Korea. We had to use an interpreter. Her English
vocabulary consisted of "Hallelujah," "Thank You,
Jesus," and two or three other similar phrases. She
had a list of four things to do to be spiritual. I loved
her number four, which was "DO IT." We can attend ten praise and worship seminars, we can get
the best notes and the best tapes on the subject and
listen to the best authority in the world, but unless
we do it, nothing happens. DO IT. Start praising
God.

There has always been praise in the Church, but
we are living in a period of greater revelation concerning praise. I lunched one day in Australia with
Anita Ridge, wife of Mr. Don Ridge, and her mother,
Mrs. Kliminock, a dear saint of God who had come
from Poland, had known ministry in Europe with
her husband, and had pioneered works in Australia. One of the many things I asked her that day was,
"What's different about today and the former days?"

"We didn't have the revelation of praise as we
have now," she said. "We loved the Lord and we
prayed, but today it's so much easier because of the
praise. It is a different day. We didn't know it in just
the same way." There never has been a day in which
this revelation has come more strongly — that
through praising we can come quickly into God's
presence.

Many people, when they hear a person preach on

prayer with a particular emphasis, follow that lead, forgetting praise and worship. Then, somebody else comes along and teaches on another aspect of prayer. So, the people do that for a while. What we need is the combination of all the aspects of prayer. I teach on those things that I feel are lacking in the particular body where I am ministering.

I was ministering in South India. After I preached one morning on the blood of Jesus, an Indian brother said to me, "I never knew you could preach on anything but the Holy Spirit." Well, in the days when he heard me I was ministering to people who desperately needed the outpouring of the Holy Spirit. So, message after message was concerning the Holy Spirit — the infilling of the Spirit, the empowerment of the Spirit, the ministry of the Spirit, the comfort of the Holy Spirit.

When the Lord sends a ministry, it is to fill in the gaps, to stir us up in the area of need. That doesn't mean God isn't saying anything else and that we can throw away everything else we believe. We need the combination of truths so that we can flow together to the goodness of God.

Ascend the hill of God in praise!

Worship

Worship ... until the glory comes.

Worship—The Natural Progression of Praise

Awaken My Heart

Words and Music by Ruth Heflin

A......waken my heart to love and a......dore Thee, O my

Lord. Awak-en my heart to pour out be....fore Thee, O my

Lord. A..waken my heart to know Thy love and to

love Thee in re.turn. Free..........ly flow............ing from an awakened

heart.......... .

Believe me, the hour cometh, when ye shall nei-
ther in this mountain, nor yet at Jerusalem,
worship the Father.
Ye worship ye know not what: we know what
we worship: for salvation is of the Jews.
But the hour cometh, and now is, when the true
worshippers shall worship the Father in spirit
and in truth: for the Father seeketh such to
worship Him.
God is a Spirit: and they that worship Him
must worship him in spirit and in truth.

Jesus

Jesus told His disciples that He needed to go by Samaria. There He sat with a woman at the well and had a conversation. She asked Him many questions. He gave her one of the greatest revelations.

Why do I say this was one of the greatest revelations? It shows what God wants. He is seeking worshipers. **If you want to live in the glory realm, you must be a worshiper.** You must worship Him more. *"The Father seeketh such to worship Him."* That is what He wants from the Earth.

The revelation given to the Samaritan woman is now being emphasized to the Body of Christ universally by the Holy Spirit. God is seeking worshipers. We may think we have always been worshipers. Every Sunday morning we attend a "worship service." We participate in the liturgy or the form. But it is possible to be in a "worship service" and never worship.

We place on the bulletin board of the church, **"Sunday Morning WORSHIP 11 AM."** The truth is that we usually have most everything but worship in our "worship" service. We call the whole service "worship." Relatively few hearts are sincerely lifted up in worship during our services. God is looking for worshipers.

Worship helps us to get rid of a lot of life's spiritual and natural frustrations. Through worship God brings to us a wholeness of body, mind and spirit. God is refining our understanding of true worship. True worship comes from the heart, in love and adoration unto the Lord.

Earlier, the Spirit of God was bringing forth the praise message. And praise is essential. It is the means of entering into the presence of the Lord. We enter His gates with singing, and we enter His courts with praise. Praise is the entering in. But in the past, once we had gotten in, we often didn't know what to do next. We either did nothing or we changed the order of the service to something like taking the offering or making the announcements.

It is much like a visit to the White House to meet the President. You might make every effort to get there, going through all the proper channels to get permission. When it is finally granted, you drive up to the White House, noticing the beauty of the entrance. After a few moments, you are ushered into the Oval Office. You look around a bit, then say, "Okay, we can go home now. I just wanted to see what it looks like."

Would you walk out of the White House without taking advantage of the opportunity to meet the President? Yet, that is what we do to God. We make an effort to come into His presence. But once we arrive, we just look around and say, "That was nice. Bye now. We'll see You next time." Why have we come? Is it not to worship the King in all of His glory, in all of His majesty?

The Lord lets us know that there is no particular place where one must worship. "Houses of God" are built, and that's fine. I like to worship God in a church building, a place of worship, a place dedicated and set apart to meet with God.

We are worshiping in a chapel adjoining our house in Jerusalem. Prior to this, we worshiped in our house. The glory came down there. If I have a choice, however, I prefer a separate place, dedicated to the Lord. This may contradict those who are promoting worship in houses. But the essential thing is not the place where we worship. A heart can meet with God anywhere one wants to meet with Him, and at any time. You can meet Him on an airplane. You can meet Him at the office, sitting at your desk.

Most of us spend very little quality time in the presence of the Lord. Yes, we pray for the nations. Yes, we ask God to bless His servants. We pray for our church programs. We believe God for "the people up the street" to get saved. But when it comes to Him and Him alone, we just don't have the time.

The Lord will have a people who worship Him. What are we to do throughout the endless ages of eternity? We are to praise and worship and adore Him. Let's begin now.

I see the difference between praising and worshiping as if I were part of the Palm Sunday procession. I join others as we take our coats off and exuberantly throw them down so the Lord can ride over them. We pluck off palm branches and wave them, even strewing them in His pathway. We shout with the whole crowd, "Hosanna! Hosanna! Blessed is He that cometh in the name of the Lord." That is praise.

I suddenly spot a little donkey moving along the Palm Sunday route. It continues on its way until it passes directly in front of me. It stops. Jesus, King of kings and Lord of lords, is seated on that donkey. He looks at me. He says, "Ruth, I love you." Tears stream down my cheeks as I reply, "Lord, I love You."

Now, I'm no longer waving my palm and shouting "Hosanna!" I'm bowing in worship and saying, "My Lord and my God." It seems that the crowd is no longer present. In reality, the multitude is still there all around me. Others are still waving their palms. They're still shouting "Hosanna!" But I'm totally oblivious to what is happening around me.

He looks at me, and all the love of eternity is poured into my soul. At this moment, I know how much He loves me. I know His majesty in a way I have never known it before. Nobody has to tell me He is King. I know it, and I worship Him, bowing before Him, recognizing His majesty, His regal position.

Worship is you shut away with God. In the middle of the busiest street in town, in the busiest restaurant, in the midst of the greatest activity of the day, you find little moments to be alone with the Lord. Thank God there can be many moments throughout the day in which it is just you and the Lord. Even though many things are happening around you, you can close yourself in with Him.

A number of years ago, one of our brothers had a vision in which he saw multitudes approaching the throne of God. These multitudes were coming in praise from all of the nations of the world. He wondered if there would be room for him, as well, at the throne. He found himself getting closer and closer. When he got to the throne, he fell down in worship and adoration. He glanced around and was conscious that nobody else was there. It was just him and the Lord.

How will it be when we are there as part of the future throngs before Him? It will be just as it is in true worship. Many others are there, but you don't know they're there. You are alone with the Lord before the throne.

The Lord has shown me how easy worship is. In Pentecostal circles we experienced what were commonly called "high moments in Zion" when I was a child. We had services in which the presence and glory of the Lord was manifested. Afterwards, we wondered how to do it again. We were not sure.

I was ministering throughout England in preparation for a meeting at the Royal Albert Hall in London, sponsored by Lady Astor. While I was teaching in a Pentecostal church one night on praise and worship, we experienced a glorious presence of God. The pastor said to me afterwards, "Only one thing worries me, Sister Ruth. How do we reproduce it?"

I think every pastor has experienced that same feeling many times. Every song leader has experienced that feeling. "We were successful tonight. That song was anointed. The glory came! Can we do it again the next time?" Because a particular song was anointed in the service last night, the song leader tries the same song the next time, and it falls flat. God allows this to happen to show us that the glory is not in a song. **The glory is in His presence.** The glory is His presence. When a pastor has had a particularly blessed service, he will often try to do it exactly the same way again, and it doesn't work.

Now, God is teaching us the secrets of His pattern for worship. If we flow in His pattern, no matter what song we sing, it will bring the glory. We can experience the glory in every service.

One of the first secrets of worship is how it differs from praise. When I praise the Lord, I *will* to praise. When I come into the house of the Lord, I offer my lips and I *will* to praise. But you do not *will* to worship. The spirit of worship must come into a meeting, must come upon you, and then you worship.

It helps to sing songs that are not very complicated. Spiritual things are easy. If your mind has to be so involved with words, you're too busy thinking. Your spirit doesn't ascend. We want our spirits to ascend in praise as the anointing increases.

Use a simple chorus. Don't worry about the beauty of the words and ideas. Don't worry about complicated thoughts. Let the choir sing those complicated numbers. Let the congregation praise and worship and adore in simplicity so that one can be lost in worship.

Overhead projectors are a blessing for visitors who may not know the choruses being used. If the congregation, however, still needs the help of the screen, then the music is too complicated for true worship. As you sing simpler songs, the spirit of worship will come.

There are more beautiful praise and worship songs available to the Body of Christ than ever before. Such a great variety. Such a wide choice. Use them to bring in the spirit of worship.

I experience it falling on my shoulders or moving in the depths of my spirit. When I do, nobody has to tell me, "Worship God." Even if we're singing the fastest songs, my spirit slows down and I'm conscious that it's only the Lord and me. I worship Him.

When a song leader is conscious that the anointing has built to the place that the spirit of worship comes, he should slip quickly into a little song of worship. It should be less wordy than the songs of praise. When you worship, you don't need to say great things. You ladies may talk on and on with your husbands — about the kids, the bills and the other affairs of your daily life. But when you have a tender moment, I'm sure the words are few and from the heart.

Now, you're not talking about the bills. You're not talking about the problems. You're not talking about the groceries. You're not talking about the children going to school. You're just enjoying each other's presence. We must do the same when we worship the Lord.

The ministry of praise increases the anointing in the service. It increases the anointing in the individual. But the ministry of worship brings the glory. Praise brings the anointing to worship, and worship brings that anointing of glory.

Just as we praise until the worship comes, so, if we want the glory, we worship until the glory comes. When you praise, worship comes, and if you want a great depth of worship, then you must have a great height of praise which enables you to ascend to the top of the hill.

Sometimes, when we are about a quarter of the way up the hill, we say, "Now let's sing a worship song." We sing it. We mouth the words, but does our heart worship? We try to worship before we get into the atmosphere of worship.

At other times that atmosphere comes so easily. We weep before the Lord. We worship Him in depth. We feel His majesty. We feel His kingliness.

With every move of God comes praise. In the past we have had a small amount of worship in proportion to the praise. That will change as revival grows. We will praise less and worship more.

When we started singing the new song, singing spontaneously, we learned a lot. We learned much about our relationship with God. We noticed that it was much easier for us to use a phrase that had a verb in it. "The Lord heals; He saves; He baptizes;

He comforts; He cares; He provides." But in worship we are focusing on the person of God, *Who* He is, not *what* He does. When we tried to worship without using the verbs, we experienced great periods of silence. So, we would return to our usual praise songs with action verbs. Through them we would move back into the presence of the Lord to see what He would show us. It took us time to learn to worship the *person* of the Lord.

If your relationship with your husband is one in which he makes the living, he takes out the garbage, he drives the car, he does certain errands, then it's not much of a relationship. That happens with many marriages. It is a "verb" relationship, based on what he does.

Many husbands, in turn, say of their wives, "She is a wonderful cook. She keeps the house clean. She cares for the children." Before you were married, did she cook the meals? Did she clean the house? Did she take care of the kids? What was it that made you love her?

"Well, it was those blue eyes."

Have you forgotten that she still has those blue eyes?

"Well, it was that smile."

Have you forgotten that she still has that smile?

"There was something wonderful and scintillating in her personality."

Women forget what made them fall in love with their husbands, too.

"Oh, it was the way he stood. There was just something about him. I could feel his strength." That was the way she thought of him before they were married. Afterwards, she thinks only of what he does. He thinks only of what she does.

It is the same in our relationship with the Lord. When we first met Him, He hadn't done anything for us that we were aware of. But we saw that He was wonderful. "Oh, I love Him with all my heart," new converts are prone to say.

After we're saved a while, we think about Him in a different way: "He saved me. He filled me with the Holy Ghost. He heals me when I'm sick." But what about Him as a *person*?

"Well, when I needed Him to pay my bills, He gave me money." But what about the Lord as a *person*?

Our praise is verb-orientated. We forget *Who* He is. If we fell in love with Him, not knowing Him, shouldn't knowing Him bring a greater relationship of love and worship? The angels in Heaven worship, and they have never been redeemed. They worship because of the *person* of the Lord. They worship because they know Him, not because they've been saved, healed, or filled with the Holy Ghost.

I'm not minimizing praising God for what He does. We should never fail to do it. I'm only stressing that God wants us also to know Him, Who was, Who is, and Who is to come, to feel His presence, to come into His presence in such a way that we will worship Him in the beauty of holiness at His holy hill. His will is for us to seek to be worshipers above all else.

I was interviewed in England by a man who works with the English Parliament, and who travels to the European Parliament and to the parliaments of other individual European countries. Having heard a little of what God had done for me, he asked me, "What are your aspirations for the future?"

I thought he was referring to our upcoming meeting at the Royal Albert Hall. So I answered, "We are believing that as the people come, and as they lift up their voices in praise, and as they worship in the Spirit, a great cloud of glory will come over the Royal Albert Hall, over all London, and over all England. We believe that it will bless and change the nation and bring forth revival."

"No! No!" he said. "I didn't mean to ask what your aspirations are in regard to this meeting. I want to know, since you've had so many wonderful experiences in life and met so many wonderful people ... [He elaborated along this line.] What are your personal aspirations for the future?"

"I just want to be a worshiper," I told him, "and I want God to give me the ability to impart the desire to worship to others."

I meant it. If the Father is seeking worshipers, then you and I need to be those who respond to the heart of the Father and worship Him in spirit and in truth. Don't let a day go by without worshiping Him.

Within the Charismatic movement, those of us with the Protestant background tend to be wonderful at praising, but most of us are not very strong worshipers. The Catholics know how to worship, but they haven't been very vibrant praisers. They need to learn how to praise. And we need to learn how to worship. As they learn how to praise and we learn how to worship, together we are coming forth in tremendous strength.

It is worship that brings forth the glory, and God's ultimate desire is that the glory of the Lord *"cover the earth as the waters cover the sea."* The glory will descend as snow. The praisers praise until the spirit of worship comes forth. The worshipers worship until the glory is manifested.

We can bring the glory in on our voices. We can bring the glory into our services, into our houses, into a community, into a city, on our voices. First we yield our voices in praise, then we yield our voices in worship, and finally the glory of God is revealed on our voices. We are learning the sweet yieldings to God.

My mother stood up in the midst of a morning teaching I was giving at winter campmeeting in Virginia and began to prophesy. She saw a vision of this last-day revival. God showed her that the last-day revival would be greater than anything the Church has seen since the crucifixion and resurrection. That's powerful, isn't it? Greater than Azusa Street. Greater than the 1948 Revival. Greater than the Day of Pentecost. Pentecost was the firstfruits. Now we're ready for the harvest. I believe we're on the verge of that revival, in the beginnings of that day in God. The way to enter into that revival is through praise and worship.

No book has been written on what God is about to do. Nobody has been this way before, to tell us, "You turn right, then left, and now go straight." We will know which way to turn if we have been in His presence in the Spirit, if we have learned to be comfortable with Him, confident and at ease.

Worship God!

Worshiping the King — Majesty

I Long to See the Face of My Savior

Vs. 1 & Cho. – Ruth Heflin
Vs. 2 & 3 — Lois Irwin

Ruth Heflin

Who is this King of glory? The Lord strong and mighty, the Lord mighty in battle.

David

When we begin worshiping, some of the first visions we have are of the feet of the Lord. Vision often begins at His feet. When we see His feet, we worship at His feet, we wash His feet with our tears, we pour out perfumed ointment upon His feet. We worship at His throne. We begin to know Him in His kingly position.

> *And immediately I was in the spirit: and, behold, a throne was set in heaven, and one sat on the throne.*
>
> *And he that sat was to look upon like a jasper and a sardine stone: and there was a rainbow round about the throne, in sight like unto an emerald.*
>
> *And round about the throne were four and*

twenty seats: and upon the seats I saw four and twenty elders sitting, clothed in white raiment; and they had on their heads crowns of gold.

And out of the throne proceeded lightnings and thunderings and voices: and there were seven lamps of fire burning before the throne, which are the seven Spirits of God.

And before the throne there was a sea of glass like unto crystal: and in the midst of the throne, and round about the throne, were four beasts full of eyes before and behind.

And the first beast was like a lion, and the second beast like a calf, and the third beast had a face as a man, and the fourth beast was like a flying eagle.

And the four beasts had each of them six wings about him; and they were full of eyes within: and they rest not day and night, saying, Holy, holy, holy, Lord God Almighty, which was, and is, and is to come.

And when those beasts give glory and honour and thanks to him that sat on the throne, who liveth for ever and ever,

The four and twenty elders fall down before him that sat on the throne, and worship him that liveth for ever and ever, and cast their crowns before the throne, saying,

Thou art worthy, O Lord, to receive glory and

honour and power: for thou hast created all
things, and for thy pleasure they are and were
created. Revelation 4:2-11

John saw the people of God again and again as
worshipers. In this passage he saw the living crea-
tures worshiping God. He saw the four and twenty
elders casting down their crowns before the Lord.
They were worshiping. He heard them calling out,
"Thou art worthy to receive glory and honor."

As late as the last chapter he said:

And I John saw these things, and heard them.
And when I had heard and seen, I fell down to
worship before the feet of the angel which
shewed me these things.
Then saith he unto me, See thou do it not: for I
am thy fellowservant, and of thy brethren the
prophets, and of them which keep the sayings
of this book: worship God.

Revelation 22:8-9

After being caught up in the glory, seeing all the
things that will be, having the greatest insights of
any man of his generation, John received the simple
message, *"Worship God."*

By this time, he should have had a Ph.D. in revelation. Why the simple message, *"Worship God"*?

After all, that's so basic. Aren't we worshiping God already? We get so caught up in complexities that we forget that God's message is the simplicity of worshiping Him.

He is willing to teach us by His Spirit how to be worshipers. He is willing to let His Spirit move upon us to enlarge us more and more so that what we offer Him is acceptable in His sight.

One day, all nations will gather in Jerusalem to worship the Lord, the King of kings and Lord of lords. I want to be there on that day.

The activity that John witnessed was, *"round about the throne," "out of the throne," "before the throne,"* and *"in the midst of the throne."*

Most Christians know only one scripture about the throne of God. If you ask them to quote something, they respond with:

> *Let us therefore come boldly unto the throne of grace, that we may obtain mercy, and find grace to help in time of need.*   Hebrews 4:16

At prayer time we say, "Let us boldly come before the throne of grace and make our petitions and requests known before the Lord." We are oriented to petitions and requests. There is a realm in God so great that, even though you may have come with a dozen petitions and requests, after worship, when

He asks, "Was there something you wanted to say to Me?" you reply, "No, Lord."

"Was there something you wanted to ask Me?"

"No, Lord!" No questions, no requests, no petitions. Everything has been satisfied.

In His presence, the things that seemed big to us become so insignificant. We wonder why we let the devil fight us over that thing, make it so important, and magnify it so much.

When we're in God's presence, the things we think are so insignificant become big. He shows us His true concerns. He lets us know, "I really am concerned about Israel. Israel is not at the bottom of My list. I really am concerned about China. I want it to be at the top of your list."

There is a greater change that comes about through worship than through any other means. If you want to be changed, worship is the key. When you are worshiping, you look into His face, and you are changed from glory to glory. We become like that which we worship. We become like Him whom we worship.

I can sit down and read every book on holiness, and I might develop some concept. But I can worship for a minute and feel His holiness and know what it is. Not only that, I can study about holiness and may get angry while I am doing it; but I worship and desire to be like Him.

> *Then David the king stood up upon his feet,*
> *and said, Hear me, my brethren, and my peo-*
> *ple: As for me, I had in mine heart to build an*
> *house of rest for the ark of the covenant of the*
> *LORD, and for the footstool of our God, and had*
> *made ready for the building.*
>
> 1 Chronicles 28:2

The place of worship is the footstool of the Lord.
We will go into his tabernacles: we will wor-
ship at his footstool.   Psalm 132:7

Some people haven't yet come into praise in spite
of the revival of praise we have experienced in the
past thirty years. God is bringing them into praise.
Some people haven't moved into the worship revelation yet. So, the Lord is teaching them. Some of
us are hungry for the glory. Glory is God's revelation for now. We are ready to worship at His
footstool.

Every service needs both praise and worship. We
praise until the spirit of worship comes, and then
we worship until the glory comes. Praise brings an
increase of the anointing. But worship brings the
majesty of God into the midst of the people. Praise
is usually more exuberant, more wordy. Worship
has that holy hush, is awesome, is less wordy. Some-

times it is even without words. In those moments, we pour out our hearts to the Lord in total silence.

The twenty-fourth psalm says, *"And the King of glory shall come in."* After you have lifted up your gates and you have lifted up the everlasting doors, the King of Glory comes in. Of whom is the psalm speaking? It is very clear: *"The Lord ... The Lord strong and mighty, the Lord mighty in battle. The Lord of hosts, He is the King of glory."* When we praise and worship, He comes in.

We know Him as Savior. We know Him as Healer. We know Him as Baptizer in the Holy Spirit. We know Him as Provider, Jehovah Jireh. We know Him in other capacities. Now it is time to know Him as King of Glory. Every experience in God has one purpose, and that purpose is to know Him.

We live by faith, totally dependent upon the Lord for our daily needs, not because we can't find another way to finance ourselves. We could. We live by faith because we want to know Him as Provider. We want that constant reassurance that He is watching over the affairs of our lives.

When we trust Him as Healer, it is not that there are no other options. There are. But we want to know Him as Healer.

And we are coming to know Him as the King of Glory.

The great image that you see in the book of Revelation is of the King of Glory coming for His glorious Church. He is coming for a Church that knows Him as the King of Glory. He fights our battles. He is the Lord of Hosts, mighty in battle. It is only in the realm of glory that we can live in the place where He fights all our battles for us.

> *And he had in his right hand seven stars: and out of his mouth went a sharp twoedged sword: and his countenance was as the sun shineth in his strength.*　　　　Revelation 1:16

Give Him the struggles and the problems. He is able to deal with them. Know the King in His power.

Canada has such a close relationship with England. The young son of a Canadian pastor friend loves the royal family so much. He has studied the family extensively. Every birthday and every Christmas his parents give him another calendar, another quarterly update of the royal family, complete with prized photographs. They are very expensive, but his love is so great that his parents wouldn't dare disappoint him.

We have an even greater privilege. It is given unto us to know the King and to know His Kingdom. It is given unto us to know everything that pertains to the King and the Kingdom. You can be familiar with the palaces of Heaven and the courts of the Lord much as a person in England would be familiar with Buckingham Palace, Windsor Castle, and Balmoral, the summer home of the royal family. It is given unto us to know the mysteries of the Kingdom of God.

So many times, when we speak about having the keys of the kingdom, we get oriented toward action. True, there are keys of the Kingdom that bring forth action:

> *Whatsoever thou shalt bind on earth shall be bound in heaven.* Matthew 16:19

But we must be oriented toward the King and the Kingdom, not only toward the works of the Kingdom.

I have had some wonderful experiences with royalty. There is something very awe-inspiring and mysterious about their position.

God gave me the privilege twice of visiting and ministering to Emperor Haile Selassie of Ethiopia in prophecy. The second time I went, God spoke to me and said, "Ruth, I am going to honor you this time more than I did the first time." I felt I had been greatly honored the first time. The emperor had not only received me, but had later received our friend Sarah Rush, a Mennonite missionary for twenty-six years in Ethiopia.

On the second occasion, I flew in one morning and

had to fly out the next morning. My friends said, "Ruth, you're foolish, arriving and expecting to see the emperor in one day, when he doesn't even know you're coming."

All I could say was, "This was the schedule God gave me. I could only get in on this plane and get out on the plane tomorrow morning in order to meet His schedule." I had to be in Jerusalem for Jewish New Year.

In spite of their doubts I called the palace and spoke to the palace minister, His Excellency Teferawerk. He said, "I'm sorry, but the emperor has a meeting with the Council of Ministers." And he began to list all the other meetings that he had that day.

I said, "Your Excellency, kindly see what you can do."

In the afternoon, I was summoned to the Palace. The first time I had gone to the Grand Palace, to the audience chamber where the emperor received heads of state, ambassadors and diplomats. This time he invited me to Jubilee Palace, his home. It was just as grand as the Grand Palace, but gone was the pomp and circumstance. I was very honored to be treated in this intimate way. We sat and talked as old friends face-to-face. His little dog, Lou Lou, a Chihuahua, was there. Lou Lou and I played together. By the way, Lou Lou was honored to be the only dog ever allowed into Disneyland.

The emperor said to me, "Ruth, when God gives you a word for any head of state, don't hesitate to go and deliver it." I felt that was probably one of the greatest indications I received of how my visit had ministered to him.

I was one of the last people who ministered to him before the troubles came. In the prophecy, God forewarned him of what was about to happen and gave him an answer.

In the presence of a king, there is a great sense of majesty and awe.

> *And when I saw him, I fell at his feet as dead.*
> *And he laid his right hand upon me, saying*
> *unto me, Fear not; I am the first and the last:*
> *I am he that liveth, and was dead; and, behold,*
> *I am alive for evermore, Amen; and have the*
> *keys of hell and of death.* Revelation 1:17-18

There was a wonderful song that came out of the revival of the fifties:

> *Behold what manner of man is this*
> *That stands between God and man?*
> *His eyes are as a flame of fire.*
> *His fan is in His hand.*

John saw Him in the seven churches
As the sun in brilliancy.
Behold! What manner of man is this?
What manner of man is He?

Chorus:
He's the Lord of Glory.
He is the great I Am.
The Alpha and Omega,
The Beginning and the End.
His name is Wonderful.
The Prince of Peace is He.
He's the Everlasting Father
Throughout eternity.   — Phyllis Speers

The King is awesome. Serving the King, however, is not something to be feared. I don't understand why we think the will of God always has to be something difficult. Many Christians are so confused on this point that if something is hard, they think it must be the will of God.

Serving the King is a joy. I have been so blessed. The will of God has been delightsome. It has been pleasurable. True, one day I have been in a palace, the next day I may have been sleeping on a dung floor in some remote village. Both experiences were equally rewarding. When you go as ambassador for the King of Kings, life's circumstances matter not.

The King of Glory deserves a chosen generation. He deserves a royal priesthood. He deserves a holy nation. He deserves a peculiar people. He deserves *"that ye should shew forth the praises of him who hath called you out of darkness into his marvellous light"* (1 Peter 2:9). Bow down before Him.

Worship the King!

Worshiping the Beloved — Intimacy

I Look Upon Your Face

Words and Music by Ruth Heflin

I look upon Your face, and wor..ship You, my Lord. I look up...on Your face, and .... wor.........ship You, my Lord

Verse 2: I worship You, my Lord.

Let him kiss me with the kisses of his mouth:
for thy love is better than wine.
Because of the savour of thy good ointments
thy name is as ointment poured forth, there-
fore do the virgins love thee.

Solomon

In the early days of my developing a relationship with the Lord in worship, I frequently saw His feet as I bowed before Him. That seemed to be the extent of my faith in worship; but as my faith increased, He didn't leave me there at His feet. Little by little the relationship grew, until I stood in His presence and saw Him face-to-face.

We begin by knowing Him as King. That in itself is glorious. But He wants to take us further. He wants us to know Him, not only as King, but as Heavenly Bridegroom. He wants us to know Him as the Beloved, the Lover of our souls, and He whom our souls love.

When we worship, we pour out our hearts to Him. We pour out our love to Him. The deep recesses of our hearts are moved by Him. We in the Western world hesitate to let our emotions show. We continually suppress them until they need to be reawakened. God wants every one of your senses to be alive unto Him. He wants you to be thrilled with the sound of His voice. He wants you to be thrilled with the touch of His hand. He wants you to be thrilled at the sight of His countenance. He wants you to be deeply moved by His presence, as He comes near.

When people are beginning to worship, and they find themselves not moved as they should be by God's presence, I encourage them to do a little fasting. Fasting decreases the natural and increases one's sensitivity to the Spirit. One develops a keenness. It restores and releases those sensitivities that we have suppressed again and again.

When the breath of the Holy Ghost blows across you, there should be an immediate response on your part. "I love You, Lord. I worship You. I adore You." Let your mouth become the pen of a ready writer. Pour out your soul to Him.

You may feel that everyone else can worship better than you. Everyone else seems to be so eloquent, so articulate, while you struggle with your inhibitions. That's not true. Maybe they can make a better pizza than you. They might do better on a particular job than you. But your worship is distinctive. It is uniquely "YOU." It touches the heart of God. He longs to hear YOUR words of love, the expression of YOUR heart, the groanings of YOUR spirit. Even if it comes forth in very simple utterances, even in sighs, don't compare yourself with others. God desires YOUR worship.

Your husband married you because he loved you. It wasn't because there were not millions of other women. His heart was drawn to you. In like manner, God's heart is drawn to us individually, as if there were no one else in the world. You may say, "He has all those other Christians who love Him." But He's not satisfied unless YOU are pouring out YOUR love to Him. You can't expect some sister in the choir to do your worshiping for you. You must do it yourself. He is waiting for YOU.

Cry out in His presence, not from pain but from ecstasy. He wants us to know the ecstasies of this intimate relationship with Him. Worship and adore Him. Bow down before Him. The Father seeketh worshipers.

As worshipers, we need to get to know that great worship book, the Song of Songs. Get to know it until it becomes part of you. After a while, it will almost feel as if you wrote it. Solomon just got a little ahead of you and put it on paper.

At first you may feel that you wish you had the ability to write it. Then later, as you enter more and more into worship, you will know you could have written it because you will have those same experiences — where God causes the lips *"of one who is asleep"* to speak. God will open your heart and touch the depths of your being in exactly that way.

In Hebrew we call this book *Shir Hash-shirim,* "the Song of Songs," instead of "the Song of Solomon." Don't be afraid of its words:

> *Let him kiss me with the kisses of his mouth:*
> *for thy love is better than wine.*
> *Because of the savour of thy good ointments thy*
> *name is as ointment poured forth, therefore do*
> *the virgins love thee.*   Song of Songs 1:2-3

Recently, archaeologists digging in Israel found a two-thousand-year-old bottle with the oil still in it. They reported that the oil was like honey in consistency, and they are sure this was the type of oil used for the priestly anointing.

We usually imagine the holy anointing oil as thin. It was thick, gooey, heavy and sticky. What wonderful oil! *"Thy name is as ointment poured forth."*

Fall in love with Jesus so much that you will be careful when you say His name. Always say it with love and fullness of expression. Sometimes the greatest worship is just whispering "Jesus," just saying His name and letting the fragrance of His name fill your soul. I have been in meetings in which God's fragrance has suddenly filled an auditorium. He has walked among us as we said His name.

Once I was in such a meeting. Suddenly, it seemed that somebody had opened the most expensive perfume and poured it out. It was something that Paris would never be able to duplicate. When the fragrance filled the room, there was a sense of the glory of God. It was beautiful.

Several years ago, Sister Janet Saunders Wheeler and I went together to the Church of the Holy Sepulchre in Jerusalem on Good Friday. Holy Week is very special in Jerusalem, even more special than Christmas in Bethlehem. We often are present for the footwashing service on Thursday in the courtyard, but we don't always go on Good Friday because the crowds are so unbelievable. That day, I worked my way through the crowd up to the "anointing stone" where, according to tradition, they laid Jesus (when they had taken Him down from the cross) to anoint Him and put spices on His body before burial. What I saw there was deeply moving. Humble pilgrims from Cyprus, Rhodes, Crete and Greece, as well as Jerusalem, had each come with a bottle of precious perfume. I watched them approach the anointing stone, take off the stoppers, and pour out the perfume without reservation to the last drop.

Some took flowers, crushed the petals, and spread

them around. There were roses and carnations, and other flowers, blending their various fragrances.

The worshipers were weeping. My non-liturgical background did not prepare me for such a sight. But my spirit was deeply touched. I stood there for hours weeping. I thought, "Jesus, in all my years of serving You, I have never witnessed such love poured out upon You by so many people at the same time." I was only sorry that I hadn't known in advance so that I too could have taken a bottle of perfume to pour out unto the Lord.

Last Good Friday we were very busy. Several tour groups had been in town the week before. We had services both Friday morning and Friday evening. I kept thinking all day that I would like to get down to the Church of the Holy Sepulchre. But I didn't make it.

When Sister Paracleta (a humble nun from a kingly Nigerian family) came to the Easter sunrise service, I realized that I hadn't seen her that week.

"Honey, where have you been?" I asked.

"*O, mama mia,*" she exclaimed excitedly in Italian (she lived and studied in Rome for a time), "I have been at the Church of the Holy Sepulchre all during Holy Week. I stayed there at night and prayed night and day."

She could hardly contain her excitement as she continued, "Do you remember the perfume you brought us when you came back from your last trip to America? I kept mine. I didn't use a drop of it. I took it down to the anointing stone on Friday. I was so thrilled to have perfume to offer the Lord. I pulled the stopper off and poured out that whole bottle of perfume."

I was glad that someone I knew had poured it out. I felt as if I should have been there pouring out my own.

When you and I worship, we are unstopping our bottles of perfume and pouring them out. Let's not be in any way skimpy, just giving Him a dab or two. Let's be lavish. Let's be generous. Let's let love flow out of the depths of our beings. Let's worship Him with words and songs of love. He is worthy! Worship Him!

What do you want to be? I want to be a worshiper.

What are your aspirations for the future? I want to be a worshiper.

What is the Father seeking? The Father is seeking worshipers.

God will teach us how to worship. He will anoint us unto worship. He will create worship within us. He will touch the depths of our beings and allow us to be those who truly worship Him in spirit and in truth.

Once, when I was ministering to Catholic friends in England on this subject, one of them said, "It amazes me that you emphasize the Song of Songs and the book of Revelation. These were the two books that the great saints of earlier centuries, the fathers of the Church, were familiar with. Many people don't read the Song of Songs because they don't understand it, and many people read the book of Revelation only from the standpoint of the woes and the end-time events, rather than from the aspect of the glory."

The Song of Songs is not an allegory. If you have ever read a love letter or a dialogue in which you saw:

He said, "..."
She said, "..."
He said, "..."
She said, "..."
He said, "..."
She said, "..."

... and then a comment on what he said, and on what she said, you shouldn't have any problem with this book. It is the love poem of the Bridegroom for the Bride and of the Bride for the Bridegroom.

Some say, "I can't even read words like that. They're too intimate." There was a brother in our fellowship who always flinched when I taught on the Song of Songs. Those tender words embarrassed him.

Would the Lord say, *"Thou art My love, thou art My dove?"* he wondered. He wasn't the only one who would have difficulty reading those words aloud. Then the Lord began to give him a new and beautiful experience. He began to prophesy in poetry. He had probably never read much poetry before that. Yet, his prophetic utterance came forth in beautiful poetic form. He would sit and weep, overcome by the beauty that God was bringing forth from his rough lips.

God wants you to have that ability to speak words of love to Him. I'm sure that most of us have not spoken to Him as tenderly as He would like. Let's do that in the days to come. Reading Song of Songs will help you. It will enlarge your ability to worship and adore. It will give you an ability to tell the Lord how much you love Him. Some of the descriptions of the Lord found there are so beautiful.

> *A bundle of myrrh is my wellbeloved unto me;*
> *he shall lie all night betwixt my breasts.*
> *My beloved is unto me as a cluster of camphire*
> *in the vineyards of En-gedi.*
> *Behold, thou art fair, my love; behold, thou art*
> *fair; thou hast doves' eyes.*
> *Behold, thou art fair, my beloved, yea, pleas-*
> *ant: also our bed is green.*   1:13-16

As the apple tree among the trees of the wood, so is my beloved among the sons. I sat down under his shadow with great delight, and his fruit was sweet to my taste.   2:3

The voice of my beloved! behold, he cometh leaping upon the mountains, skipping upon the hills.
My beloved is like a roe or a young hart: behold, he standeth behind our wall, he looketh forth at the windows, shewing himself through the lattice.   2:8-9

Who is this that cometh out of the wilderness like pillars of smoke, perfumed with myrrh and frankincense, with all powders of the merchant?
     3:6

What is thy beloved more than another beloved, O thou fairest among women? what is thy beloved more than another beloved, that thou dost so charge us?
My beloved is white and ruddy, the chiefest among ten thousand.
His head is as the most fine gold, his locks are bushy, and black as a raven.
His eyes are as the eyes of doves by the rivers of waters, washed with milk, and fitly set.

> *His cheeks are as a bed of spices, as sweet flow-*
> *ers: his lips like lilies, dropping sweet smelling*
> *myrrh.*
>
> *His hands are as gold rings set with the beryl:*
> *his belly is as bright ivory overlaid with sap-*
> *phires.*
>
> *His legs are as pillars of marble, set upon sock-*
> *ets of fine gold: his countenance is as Lebanon,*
> *excellent as the cedars.*
>
> *His mouth is most sweet: yea, he is altogether*
> *lovely. This is my beloved, and this is my friend,*
> *O daughters of Jerusalem.*   5:9-16

There is a purpose in all of this. He wants you to look upon His face. He wants you to see His eyes. He wants you to see His cheeks. He wants you to know Him in ways you have not known Him until now.

The Jews believe that the Song of Songs was given at the dedication of the Temple. Some say that the Song was more important than the Temple. Although it is a short book, it has been such a blessing to us.

If you have cassette tapes of the Bible, find the one with the Song of Songs on it. Put it in the tape deck in your car and listen to it again and again. Let it get into your spirit. Then, when you worship, you will find you have a new depth of expression.

God wants to awaken your heart to love. He wants to awaken your heart to adoration. He wants to awaken in you the ability to worship Him.

I have been in many churches throughout China and have discovered that they are the only churches in the world where when you say to the people, "Let us pray," everybody in the building prays. They don't pray audibly, but you can see the spirit of prayer on them. How beautiful to see an entire congregation, with nobody looking around, nobody daydreaming or planning the menu for tonight's supper, or making any other plans. They pray. They are lost in prayer.

True worship is like that. We must be able to go home from the house of the Lord and know that at some point in the service we have poured out our hearts in love and adoration and worship before Him. If we make up our minds that we'll never go to the house of the Lord without pouring out the depths of our spirits to Him in worship, He will be pleased. He delights in a people who delight in Him — not just in what He does for us — but in who He is.

Worship is an attitude of the heart in which the heart bows down before God. No one else is present. There are no thoughts in your mind other than of God. You haven't come with a petition. You haven't come with a request. You haven't come because you need healing. You haven't come because of some other need. You have come because you love Him so much and you feel the need to express that love. **Worship is a time of love.** He pours out His love on us, and we pour out our love to Him.

The waiting Bride of the Song of Songs does not say, "I love Him because He has healed me; He saved me; He delivered me; He set me free; He brought me a long way; He led me; He guided me." She says, *"This is my Beloved. This is my Friend."*

The Lord wants us to know Him so intimately that we can present Him to others and can describe Him — from personal experience, from having seen Him, from having heard His voice, from having felt His touch.

For years I have led people in praise over the microphone. The first time I tried to lead in public worship, I felt so inhibited. Worship is so intimate. I felt naked and bare in front of the congregation. I thought, "I can never do this." The Lord reminded me that if I wouldn't, then who would help teach the people how to worship Him in intimacy. By His grace I have continued to haltingly lead in public worship. We are all relaxing more in His presence.

Some of the most beautiful expressions of love have come from young people, from young believers. *"Out of the mouths of babes and sucklings"* we have heard God perfecting praise. Their love for the Lord is so fresh that it is contagious. God wants each of us to love Him so much that it becomes contagious — that others will want to love Him in the same way.

When I was serving the Lord in Hong Kong as a young girl, one of the criticisms I received was that I tended to come to church "prayed up," excited about Jesus. Most of my church friends had a nine-to-five church job. Many of them felt that if they worked nine-to-five for God, they didn't want to take their work home with them. If they went out socially, they didn't want to talk about God in the evening. God was their nine-to-five job. They wanted to talk about anything else and everything else at other times. I got a lot of criticism for talking about God after working hours. I can't stop talking about Him all the time, anytime, anywhere, everywhere.

Your love of Jesus must be so contagious that others will say, "I want to love God like that person loves Him. I want a new relationship. I want to be able to describe Him as the Lover of my soul. I don't want to be inhibited in my expressions of love for the Lord." (If we can talk freely about everything else, God wants us to have the ability to speak intimately about Him.)

When the Charismatic outpouring began, I was

very blessed because I was in Hong Kong, where I had the privilege of helping to arrange meetings for men like Rev. David du Plessis, Rev. Ed Stube, and others. These men often said that the hardest words for the nominal Christian to say were "I love You, Jesus," that is, until they were filled with the Holy Ghost. After they spoke in tongues, however, these were the first words they spoke in English.

God is bringing in a new day of glory in which we are going to be able to pour out our love continually unto Him without hesitation, without any embarrassment at all. Our description of Him must be, "His mouth is most sweet. He is altogether lovely."

In the Song of Songs, He calls us into the fields. He says, *"There will I give thee My loves."* He calls us away so that we can hear His voice, that voice *"as the sound of many waters."*

Fall in love with Him. Worship Him. The more you worship Him, the more intimately you will know Him. The more intimately you know Him, the more you will want to know Him. If you really know the Lord, there is no room for indifference. If you are still tainted by indifference, you are living too close to the world. You are too involved in the things of life. The closer you live to Him, the more you will want to hear His voice. Oh, the thrill of His voice in the night season — even when He is correcting us!

Once I was driving behind the wheel. He said so plainly to me, "My ways are not your ways. My thoughts are not your thoughts." I got excited. I was being rebuked, but I was being rebuked by the Lord. Such a wonderful voice! Rebuked by the Lord! I didn't mind that at all.

"Speak to me, Lord, even if it is Your loving rebuke." I got excited that day.

"My ways are not your ways. My thoughts are not your thoughts."

I thought I was getting pretty good at knowing His ways and His thoughts.

"My ways are not your ways. My thoughts are not your thoughts."

His ways are higher. His thoughts are higher. He continually calls us from the earthly to the heavenly, from the natural to the supernatural. Oh, the sound of His voice! He can rebuke me anytime.

As Americans, one of our problems is that we hear too many sounds. We hear too many voices. There are even too many ministry sounds. I tell people jokingly (because I have my own tapes available) that I want to produce an audiotape entitled "Learning to Know the Voice of God" and sell it all over America. When you put it in your tape player, it would be totally silent for an entire hour. "Learning to Know the Voice of God" — one hour of silence, making it possible for us to hear God!

Those of us who have lived overseas often have found ourselves in places where we have had no one to talk to. I have traveled on trains, buses, and planes when there was no one else who spoke English. People were conversing in their own languages. So, I learned to commune with the Lord.

In the United States you are barraged with sound continually. You must learn to tune in to the gentle voice of the Savior. *"His voice is as the sound of many waters."* Oh, the thrill of His voice! There can be no greater thrill in all the world. If we turn a deaf ear to His voice, if we suppress the hearing of His voice, if we don't appreciate His voice and would rather hear something else, He will go somewhere else and speak to someone else. But if we love the sound of His voice, He will talk to us often.

Have you ever called someone to say, "I miss the sound of your voice"? Have you ever gotten in the presence of the Lord and said to Him, "Let me hear Your voice; I am not asking You to tell me that I am good; I am not asking You to tell me that I am wonderful; I am not even asking You to tell me something to do or someplace to go; I just want to hear Your voice"? You should do it. He is waiting to hear it.

In delight, the Bride of the Song of Songs says:

The voice of my beloved! behold, he cometh leap-ing upon the mountains, skipping upon the hills. 2:8

He speaks so tenderly to us in return:

Thou hast ravished my heart, my sister, my spouse; thou hast ravished my heart with one of thine eyes, with one chain of thy neck.
How fair is thy love, my sister, my spouse! how much better is thy love than wine! and the smell of thine ointments than all spices!
Thy lips, O my spouse, drop as the honeycomb: honey and milk are under thy tongue; and the smell of thy garments is like the smell of Leba-non.
A garden inclosed is my sister, my spouse; a spring shut up, a fountain sealed.
Thy plants are an orchard of pomegranates, with pleasant fruits; camphire, with spikenard,
Spikenard and saffron; calamus and cinnamon, with all trees of frankincense; myrrh and aloes, with all the chief spices:
A fountain of gardens, a well of living waters, and streams from Lebanon. 4:9-15

I sleep, but my heart waketh: it is the voice of my beloved that knocketh, saying, Open to me, my sister, my love, my dove, my undefiled: for my head is filled with dew, and my locks with the drops of the night.   5:2

Thou art beautiful, O my love, as Tirzah, comely as Jerusalem, terrible as an army with banners.

Turn away thine eyes from me, for they have overcome me: thy hair is as a flock of goats that appear from Gilead.

Thy teeth are as a flock of sheep which go up from the washing, whereof every one beareth twins, and there is not one barren among them.

As a piece of a pomegranate are thy temples within thy locks.

There are threescore queens, and fourscore concubines, and virgins without number.

My dove, my undefiled is but one; she is the only one of her mother, she is the choice one of her that bare her. The daughters saw her, and blessed her; yea, the queens and the concubines, and they praised her.

Who is she that looketh forth as the morning, fair as the moon, clear as the sun, and terrible as an army with banners?   6:4-10

He loves us so.

It is good to compare the Lord with all the finest

things of life. I know there is no comparison, but He likes to hear us say it. You men, your wives know that they're the finest, but they like to hear you say it. They want you to remind them why they are the chosen ones. Tell the Lord why He is *"the fairest of ten thousand."*

Don't be afraid of intimacy. In the Song of Songs the relationship goes from King to Shepherd to Lover of her soul to Beloved. Get to know Him in all of these ways.

Some people get upset with God. If you must get upset, get upset with everybody else; but don't get upset with God.

When Mother and Daddy first went into the ministry, they had put all their savings into a tent and its related equipment. They both had left their jobs. During the first revival they held, a storm blew the tent down. Daddy was so upset that he decided to go back home and return to his secular work. He must have been speaking against God, because he remembered that Mother started crying and said to him, "Wallace, don't talk about Jesus like that." That touched Daddy. He was so strong and Mother was so delicate.

"If my little wife can take this setback and not be swayed, if she can take the testings, then I can too. I am a big, strong man." He never again wanted to "back up." It was my mother's words that had moved him.

If you get upset, don't speak against Jesus. In every situation He is altogether lovely. I find no fault in Him. All of His ways are high. All of His ways are holy. All of His ways are glorious.

Worship the Beloved in intimacy!

Glory

Then ... stand in the glory!

The Glory Realm

He Is So Beautiful

ANDANTE

Words and Music by Ruth Heflin

He is so beau-ti-ful, just look up-on Him_____ He is so beau-ti-ful, Heaven's di-a dem. He is so beau-ti-ful, be-hold Him and see_____ the beau-ty of Je - sus, Hea-ven's ma-jes-ty.

But we all, with open face beholding as in a glass the glory of the Lord, are changed into the same image from glory to glory, even as by the Spirit of the Lord.

Paul

What is the glory realm? It is the realm of eternity. It is the revelation of the presence of God. It is the manifestation of His presence. He is glory. He is everywhere, but glory is the manifestation of that reality. Earth has the atmosphere of air, whereas the heavenly atmosphere is glory, His presence. When glory comes down, it's a bit of Heaven's atmosphere coming down to us, a taste of His manifest presence.

We don't see the air, do we? But all of us would be dead if we were not breathing it. We are not conscious of the air unless we see the wind blowing the leaves on the trees. Yet, the Earth is covered by it. In the same way, not one inch of Heaven lacks glory. Now, God is giving us a taste of that glory, Heaven manifested on Earth.

God is revealing His glory visibly to many people.

I was speaking at Dr. Fuchsia Pickett's church in Dallas. A brother came up to me after the service and said, "Sister Ruth, as you were speaking we saw the glory as a cloud enter and begin to rise in the aisles, slowly covering the congregation. The more you spoke, the more the cloud rose. By the time you finished, it was over the heads of all the people. You were on the platform, and that glory continued to rise until all we could see was your head."

There have been times when I have spoken that people couldn't even see me. They could only see the light of the glory of God. Many times people have told me that as I was preaching they saw a cloud form like the figure of a man and stand beside me while I was ministering. The cloud has also been seen above me, beside me, behind me, in front of me, and engulfing me.

Sometimes the glory comes down as dewdrops. Sometimes it comes down as golden drops of rain. Sometimes it comes as a pillar of cloud. Sometimes it comes as a pillar of fire. Sometimes it comes as a mist. Some people see little sparkles, the glory dust that falls from His garment. Some see it as a gray or yellow smoke. People see it in many different ways. It doesn't matter exactly how you see the glory, just see it.

One of our young people in Jerusalem saw the glory and described it as a "giant marshmallow."

Well, if it looked like a marshmallow to him, that's okay. Some see the fire of God coming down as a ball of flame or tongues of fire. The vocabulary with which we describe the glory is not the important thing. Experiencing it is. Let the glory come into the midst of the people of God, the glory of His presence.

Just as we believe in created praise and created worship, we believe in created glory.

> *And the* LORD *will create upon every dwelling place of mount Zion, and upon her assemblies, a cloud and smoke by day, and the shining of a flaming fire by night: for upon all the glory shall be a defence [covering].* Isaiah 4:5

We are only beginning to see the glorious day of the Lord. God has shown us that every day we can experience the glory through the simplicity of praise and worship. It is not that we haven't had praise in the church. It is not that we haven't had worship in the church. And it's not that we haven't had glory in the church. But we haven't known how praise and worship work together to bring forth the glory.

Whether I am praying alone, with three or four other people, or with three or four thousand, if I praise and continue praising until the spirit of worship comes and continue to worship, soon the glory comes. We must spend time in worship as we have spent time in praise.

It doesn't take hours. As you learn how to flow in the Spirit, you can come quickly into the secret place, the hidden place of the stairs.

Jacob saw the ladder with the angels ascending and descending. In Hebrew, the word for ladder is *sullam.* It has a numerical value of 136. Likewise, the word for voice, *kol,* has the numerical value of 136. The voice then becomes the ladder of ascent. Angels are regularly seen in our meetings. They come because our praise and worship create the atmosphere of Heaven. Praise and worship bring the glory. The Lord both brings that glory down to us and takes us up into the glory. Are you hungry for the glory?

Don't ever think that you have gone beyond praise. Praise will always be necessary. It is the key. It is the entering in. It is the ascent. Often, people try to start off worshiping in a service. It just doesn't work the same way. God honors us because of the hunger in our hearts. But, if we want to experience deep worship, we need vibrant praise first. If we have vibrant praise, then we'll have deep worship. And we'll have the fullness of the glory of God manifested.

Perhaps you have never heard glory. Several years

ago, on an Easter Sunday in Jerusalem, we had a very full day. My brother was leaving early that morning with his tour group to cross the border to Jordan on his way back to the U.S.A. The day began for us with a sunrise service. Then, we cooked, entertained many people for breakfast, and went to see the group off. We had our Sunday service and, again, lunch in the garden. In the afternoon we went to hear a choir sing *The Messiah*. By the time we got around to the evening service, I wondered if our people would be so weary that we would not have a good service.

As we were opening the service, Karen Stage, one of our girls, gave a word. I'm not sure if it was a word of praise or a prophecy, but there was a sound of eternity in her voice that was so glorious. It brought with it a refreshing. It was as if we had all taken a month's vacation in one second. We were ready for church. She brought eternity into the meeting with her voice. It was a sound of glory that filled our souls and energized us.

If Hitler could control the masses in a negative sense by his voice, then God will have a people who have an anointing upon their voices. When they speak, the glory of God will be manifested.

Some folks were critical of Brother Roland Buck and his experiences with angels, which he related in his book, *Angels on Assignment*. When the book was first published, Mother brought a copy with her when she visited Jerusalem. As she read it aloud to me, we cried together. We were so blessed by the stories he told. She would read a little while and we would cry a little. Then, she would read a little more and we would cry a little more. We knew that it was of God.

During that time when he was getting so much criticism, somebody brought us some tapes on which he was telling the same story recounted in the book. As I listened to the tapes, I could hear the sound of eternity in his voice. I knew that heavenly sound. I knew that glory sound. I didn't even have to hear what he said. I recognized the realm of the Spirit. There is a glory sound that ministers to the depths of the spirit.

William Branham had a sound of glory in his voice.

God has used Harald Bredesen, a Spirit-filled Dutch Reformed minister, to bless many people. I was always blessed by his ministry because there was a sound of glory in his voice.

Certain people have it even when they are not praising and worshiping. They can be talking about the price of beans, about rice in China, and still they have that sound of glory on their voices.

Jesus had that sound in His voice. And God wants

to put it in our voices. We will get it as we use our voices more and more to praise and worship Him.

> *That in every thing ye are enriched by him, in all utterance, and in all knowledge.*
> 1 Corinthians 1:5

> *Grace and peace be multiplied unto you through the knowledge of God, and of Jesus our Lord, According as his divine power hath given unto us all things that pertain unto life and godliness, through the knowledge of him that hath called us to glory and virtue [excellence].*
> 2 Peter 1:2-3

It is not enough that the glory of God be revealed in China, Africa or Asia. I must live in the realm of the glory being revealed in my life. As the glory is revealed, I begin to have grace and peace multiplied unto me. The glory works in us to make us overcomers in every respect. The glory works in us to bring forth an excellence. We should be known as those who have excellent spirits and excellent ministries. The only way we can have that excellence is by knowing the realm of the glory of God.

> *For he received from God the Father honour and glory, when there came such a voice to him from*

> *the excellent glory, This is my beloved Son, in*
> *whom I am well pleased.*   2 Peter 1:17

Some of you might be thinking, "Sister Ruth, I thought that we wanted the glory so that we could see miracles of healing and deliverance." Yes, we want that too, and it comes with the glory. But not everybody is sick. Everybody does need peace and grace.

Many years ago the Lord spoke to me in Jerusalem that we should have teaching on the glory in our Bible school. I felt that I wasn't equipped to teach the subject, so I called Sister Victorine Cheek, an old-timer in Pentecost who had been a great Bible teacher for many years. She taught for us once a week. "Sister Victorine," I asked, "would you be willing to teach on the glory? God told me that He wants us to have some lessons on the subject."

She said, "Yes." Later, she had second thoughts and called back to say that she didn't think she was ready to teach on the glory.

Well, I knew that God wanted us to learn more about the glory, so I decided to teach what I knew. "I'm going to teach you everything I know on the glory," I told our folks on the first day, "and then we're going to have to believe for the revelation of God to come forth in the area of glory." That's what we did.

When you preach on salvation, folks get saved. When you preach on healing, folks get healed. When you preach concerning financial provision, folks begin to move into the provision of God. And when you preach on the glory, you begin to have a revelation of the glory of God.

God, in His faithfulness, began to teach us. As we looked into the glory, however, we found that the enemy of our souls had many diversionary tactics to try to take our eyes away from the Lord and His glory to the daily troubles of life. God gave one of our young people a chorus:

> *What shall come forth*
> *From the fire of the Lord?*
> *Only GLORY! Only GLORY!*
> *And what do we desire?*
> *Only GLORY! Only GLORY!*
> *And Who do we desire?*
> *Only JESUS! Only JESUS!*

We determined that nothing would prevent or distract us as we pressed into the glory. Now, there's hardly a time that we gather that a beautiful sense of the glory of God doesn't come into our midst.

When we initially began using the Catholic church, St. Peter-en-Gallicantu, it was such an amazing ecumenical opportunity — far beyond anything that was happening in Jerusalem at that time in this regard.

We didn't know how long we would have the privilege of worshiping on Mount Zion. We didn't know all God's purposes for us, only the beginning. So, we promised God that every night we would praise and worship Him with all that was within us. Even on very cold nights, the Lord helped us to keep that promise.

Each night we worshiped as if it were our only night on Mount Zion — although we borrowed the church for nearly ten years and still have a close relationship with the fathers.

Praise is the entering into the presence of the Lord. The spirit of worship comes as we enter into a place of great anointing.

Someone has said that we need to go deeper in order to go higher. I believe that's like the chicken and the egg question: which comes first, the chicken or the egg? I personally believe that we need to go higher in order to go deeper. In praise we ascend. The more exuberant the praise, the greater the depth of worship will be.

Praise brings the anointing, but worship brings the glory. If you want the glory in every service, there must also be worship in every service. Just as we praise until that anointing is increased, so we must worship until the glory comes.

In some services, we're able to worship longer. I like morning services because we can give ourselves to longer praise and longer worship so that the glory comes. When the glory comes, two things happen. One, the spirit of revelation begins to work in our hearts. Two, we are changed by the glory.

> *Now the Lord is that Spirit: and where the Spirit of the Lord is, there is liberty.*
> 2 Corinthians 3:17

That liberty comes forth as we are worshiping. Verse eighteen says:

> *But we all, with open face beholding as in a glass the glory of the Lord, are changed into the same image from glory to glory, even as by the Spirit of the Lord.*

Get into the glory realm and see the wonderful things that God has waiting for you.

One of the most important ingredients for having the glory revealed is unity. We found that we could be singing the same songs and dancing the same dance and not be in one spirit. And the glory doesn't come until we're in one spirit. When oneness of spirit comes, unity comes forth. When unity comes forth, immediately the glory falls. Your desire for the glory makes you willing to lay aside a lot of petty things that you fought for in the past, things that really are meaningless — in the light of eternity.

In an orchestra, the individual musicians tune their own instruments, then follow the conductor. They are not checking to make sure they are synchronized with each other. Rather, as each is synchronized with the conductor, they are automatically in time with each other. The Lord showed us that if at any given time in a service everyone is focused on the Lord, that's unity.

I like so much the phrase of the chorus:

> *Just forget about yourself*
> *And concentrate on Him*
> *And worship Him!*

One morning we all came into the prayer meeting in Bethlehem a little weary from a late meeting the night before. One brother that morning, within about two minutes, ran up the mountain of God and was already at the top waving his banner. "I'm here! I'm here!" Nobody else had reached the foot of the mountain yet.

In the old days of Pentecost, when someone got blessed, you were happy for that person, and you stood by and watched him or her get blessed. I tapped this brother on the shoulder and said, "Come back down, and let's take everyone up together."

This is not a day in which one person sees the glory and the rest of us just sit back and watch and listen. Oh, no! This is the day in which all flesh shall see it together. There is nothing more wonderful than the glory being revealed collectively to an entire congregation.

That morning the brother came back down and we continued praising, moving up slowly, until everybody began to flow together. Flowing together, we came up higher and higher. Then we began to worship, and the glory came. After a couple of hours had passed, I tapped him on the shoulder and asked, "Wasn't that better?"

"Yes," he admitted, "it's better when we all see the glory together." God is teaching us how to do it. What has happened previously individually is now happening congregationally. It was the congregational aspect of the praise that was new to the people when we first came to Jerusalem.

> *Oh that men would praise the LORD for his goodness, and for his wonderful works to the children of men!*
> *Let them exalt him also in the congregation of the people, and praise him in the assembly of the elders.* Psalm 107:31-32

Pastors, song leaders, don't be disturbed when you try to move in these ways and it doesn't always seem to work. God will teach you. Sometimes we learn more by the times we miss it. Now, at least, we're conscious that we miss it. Before, we weren't even conscious of that. We just went on in our own form of worship and liturgy.

We want the glory of God to be manifested in the midst of the people in these days. And God is helping us to know how to praise Him, to know how to worship and adore until the glory of God is revealed.

In the worship realm we are more conscious of God's quality of love. But in the glory realm we are more conscious of His holiness. This is why the angels cry, "Holy! Holy!"

> *And one cried unto another, and said, Holy, holy, holy, is the LORD of hosts: the whole earth is full of his glory.* Isaiah 6:3

When we get in the glory realm, we not only understand why the angels cry "Holy," we join them!

The glory realm is the realm of eternity!

The Glory Brings an Ease

Standing in the Glory

Words and Music by Ruth Heflin

Standing in the glo.....ry of the Lord ...., I see Him face to face ......, my blessed Lord .... Standing in the glo......ry of the Lord ...., I see Him face to face ...., my bless......ed Lord ....

Let us labour therefore to enter into that rest, lest any man fall after the same example of unbelief.

Paul

The first thing we notice about the glory realm is the ease it brings. The glory brings an ease in every dimension of ministry. The glory brings an ease, for instance, in the ministry of healing. We may have prayed for the sick in one dimension, but when we move into the glory realm, healing just happens. There is no struggle.

The glory brings ease in the area of finances. Whereas we have asked the people to give to the Lord and perhaps have had to urge them at times to do so, when the glory comes, they quickly and willingly empty their pocketbooks.

Whatever God has called us to do, in any realm of ministry, the glory brings an ease to it and takes away the struggle, the striving, the effort. It makes you feel like you are on a Holy Ghost roller coaster. You just let the King of Glory do the work.

"What do I do in life's extremities?" If you can get alone with God and begin to praise Him, then move into worship and let the glory come down, you will find yourself an overcomer. You'll find God working on your behalf.

Several years ago, when I had just returned from an overseas trip, I walked into our fellowship in Jerusalem. I have never felt the glory of God as I felt it there that day. There was an awesome sense of His presence. I have never felt such awe before or since. Many have experienced what we call the "holy hush." After great praising and rejoicing and much worship, it seems as if a conductor has brought an orchestra to a quiet moment after the crescendo and everybody stands in total quietness, feeling the majestic presence of God's glory.

That day in Jerusalem I felt it as never before. I suddenly knew how easy it is to raise the dead and to heal all manner of sickness and disease. How easy it is in that realm of glory! How easy to see people leaping out of wheelchairs and off of stretchers! How easy to see blind eyes opened and deaf ears unstopped! In that realm, nothing is impossible.

That glory must have stayed with us two or three hours. God was giving us a foretaste, as He often does, of a greater day, so that we could encourage ourselves and others to move into the glory realm.

God showed me that day that if there is no death working in me, if there is no bitterness, no strife, no criticism (nothing of death), I can command death. If death is working in me, I have no authority over death. If only life is flowing through me, I have an authority over death and I can command it in the name of the Lord. We must move into the resurrection power of God. As we live in the glory realm, we will see the miraculous such as the world has never seen.

Kathryn Kuhlman ministered in the glory realm. She just called out what she saw God doing.

William Branham ministered in the glory realm.

There are some individuals today, such as Benny Hinn, who are flowing in the glory realm. But God is going to bring forth whole congregations all over the world that will know how to move in it.

If we have learned how to praise and have become a praising people (where we weren't in the past), if we have learned how to worship and become worshiping people (where we weren't in the past), can't God bring us into being glory people with a glory anointing?

The Scriptures say:

For the earth shall be filled with the knowledge

> *of the glory of the* LORD, *as the waters cover the*
> *sea.*   Habakkuk 2:14

God is not saying that His glory will come down upon the world willy-nilly. No! God has always used earthen vessels. So, if we're going to see an increase of the glory on the Earth, it will be through people such as you and I. We must become familiar with the glory. We must experience the glory realm as never before.

All Spirit-filled children of God have the privilege of bringing the glory and the ease into a service, into their own lives, into their households, into their churches, into their communities, into their nations. We do it with our voices. The lifting up of the voice brings a different atmosphere into a place.

With the glory present, you no longer have to work at your ministry as you used to. You don't have to work at your business as you used to have to work at it. You don't have to work at your family as you used to work at it. There is a rest, an ease, in the realm of glory.

> *Let us labour therefore to enter into that rest,*
> *lest any man fall after the same example of un-*
> *belief.*   Hebrews 4:11

The apostle Paul gives us a paradox. There is a striving, a laboring. But you strive only to enter in. Once you enter in, you know the rest.

The glory brings an ease!

The Glory Brings Revelation

Let the Glory

Words and Music by Ruth Heflin

Let the glo.....ry bring forth ease, ease ..... in the glo.......ry. Let the glo....ry bring forth ease, ease in the Spir...it of God. I love Thy ways, O Lord. Thy ways are in the heavenlies. I love Thy ways, O Lord. Thy ways are in the.. cloud.

For God, who commanded the light to shine out of darkness, hath shined in our hearts, to give the light of the knowledge of the glory of God in the face of Jesus Christ.

Paul

The glory brings revelation. As His presence is manifested, you begin to see into the glory realm.

Revelation always begins with the Lord. The revelation may be simple at first as you begin to see Him. Some see only His feet. Some see only His hand. Some see His face.

Where does that *"light of the knowledge of the glory of God"* come from? It comes from the very *"face of Jesus Christ."* That's why I come into a service and begin to praise. Then, I continue into worship. Then, as I worship, I begin to look at the Lord. The glory brings an anointing to see. I am sure that many of you have never seen the face of the Lord. I can assure you that if you will worship until the glory comes, you will begin to see Him. The more you worship, and the more the glory comes, the more you will see. You will come to the place that you never worship without seeing the face of Jesus.

"The knowledge of the glory of God" comes from the *"face of Jesus Christ."* Therefore, we must be those who see His face. This is not just an added privilege for a select group of people. It is given to every one of us to have eyes that are anointed to see.

Earlier in Pentecost, we were not taught that we all could see. We believed in vision, and there were always those who were visionary. Because we were not taught to believe to see, many of us were without seeing for years. God spoke to us one day in Jerusalem and said that the whole man (in the natural) sees, hears, and feels. If someone doesn't hear, we say he is "deaf." If he hears a little, we say he is "hard of hearing." If he doesn't see at all, we say he is "blind," or if he sees only a little, we say he "sees dimly." Yet we've never been taught that we can all see in the Spirit.

God wants to take us in vision to His throne. He wants to show us the face of Jesus. In seeing Jesus, I am changed. Every time I stand in the glory, I'm changed a little more. Every time I look on His face, I have a desire to be more like Him. He is the example. It's in the glory that I see Him and desire to be like Him.

There may be a general desire to be like Him aside from the glory. But in the glory I know what it is to be like Him. I know what His compassion feels like. I know what His holiness feels like. I know what His love is like. I know what His mercy is like. In the glory I know Him in a way that I can't know Him in any other way.

The Lord wants us to be anointed to see. Anything that Ezekiel saw, you and I can see. Anything that John the Revelator saw, you and I can see. We simply haven't taught enough on seeing in the realm of the Spirit. God showed me that if people are taught, it is very easy for them to see the face of the Lord. I tried it out at summer campmeeting.

Sister Gladys Faison, who has been attending our church for fifteen or twenty years, came onto the platform weeping one night that week.

"Sister Faison, why are you crying?" I asked.

"I have been so blessed," she said. "All these years I have struggled, wanting to see the Lord. I have struggled, wanting to see the heavenlies. I have struggled, striving to enter into something eternal. This week, while we have been singing in the Spirit, I have seen the Lord every day. I have seen the heavenlies. It has all come so easily. I never knew it was so simple." Dozens of others had a similar experience.

I sometimes go into churches that have several hundred people, and none of them have ever seen the face of the Lord. As the congregation stands and worships for ten or fifteen minutes, at least fifty of them see the Lord for the first time.

Why does it happen at that moment and come so easily? Because they have been taught that they can see and they look expecting to see. When you look expecting to see, you begin to see.

> *Now the Lord is that Spirit: and where the Spirit of the Lord is, there is liberty.*
> *But we all, with open face beholding as in a glass the glory of the Lord, are changed into the same image from glory to glory, even as by the Spirit of the Lord.*   2 Corinthians 3:17-18

No matter what experience you have in God, you'll never have anything more thrilling than looking at His face. In the glory, you gradually learn how to come in and see His face more often. His face is not, then, so elusive. And you don't see it through a glass darkly, either. You see Him face-to-face.

I remember a time when I longed to see Him so. Some of my friends had seen Him face-to-face and I hadn't. I didn't know how to do it. I wish somebody had taught a seminar on the subject. I was so hungry, so very hungry, to see His face. I am so grateful that He taught me how.

I remember the days when Irene, my friend and associate, would weep because everyone else was having visions and she wasn't. Now, the spirit of revelation works so beautifully in her that it's a joy to be in a meeting with her.

If you will praise until the spirit of worship comes, and if you will worship until the glory comes, you will see the Lord. He will show Himself to you in so many wonderful ways. You'll see Him more and more clearly and you'll know Him more and more intimately — until your heart is bubbling over with so much love for Him that you could write your own Song of Songs.

For many years I couldn't understand why the Lord said so many times in Scripture, *"Seek My face."* Since becoming a worshiper, I have learned that the will of God and the purposes of God can be seen in the face of the Lord. When you are looking at His face, you know His purposes. You know His mind. You know His desires. You see His heart.

I have looked into His face and seen the harvest fields of the world. I have looked into His face and seen the map of the world.

John's experience is a good example for us. Anything he saw we can see. Nearly every chapter of Revelation contains the words *"I saw."*

> *And I turned to see the voice that spake with me. And being turned, I saw seven golden candlesticks.* Revelation 1:12

John turned to see. Thank God for the turnings that allow us to see into the glory realm. Some people are tired of change. Others are afraid of change. They say, "Don't ask me to turn further in order to see God," when maybe the slightest turn will bring them into that place of seeing. Don't be weary of personal effort when it comes to seeking God. John turned and he saw.

What did he see? He saw seven golden candlesticks. At the end of the chapter, we learn that the seven golden candlesticks are actually the seven churches. If you have a problem in seeing the Lord, know this: He will always be found among His people, in the midst of the congregation. Sometimes people who are passing through the distresses of life, when they have burdens and are severely tested, run away from the church. They run away from the religious. They run away from those they love.

"I'm fed up," they say. "I've had enough."

You will always find the Lord in the midst of the churches, no matter how imperfect they may be. That's the place He wants to be found, and that's the place He will be found. That's the place where He will be seen. He loves the Church and gave Himself for it.

It makes no difference where we meet, whether in a Gothic cathedral or in a house in the suburbs. He loves the Church and will always be found in the midst of her. If you want to see the Lord, look in the Church. John turned and saw seven golden candlesticks.

> *And in the midst of the seven candlesticks one like unto the Son of man, clothed with a garment down to the foot, and girt about the paps with a golden girdle.*
> *His head and his hairs were white like wool, as white as snow; and his eyes were as a flame of fire.* Revelation 1:13-14

I have looked into those flaming eyes. And I have felt His love as fire burning. That fire of love cannot be quenched until all of His purposes for the world are fulfilled. That passion for the souls of men and for lost humanity can never diminish. I have looked into His eyes and seen the nations of the world. I have looked into His eyes and seen His heart's cry (depending on the period of time and what was happening in the Earth).

If you want to see the heart of God, look into His eyes. You will see His heart. Knowledge and wisdom come forth from the eyes of the Lord.

You may see His mouth or other features. Then, as you wait in His presence, He may show you other things — that is, if you have time. (We don't always have time for what He wants to show us.) He may show you parts of Heaven. He may show you His beautiful rose garden, His garden of love, greater than the Gardens of Shalimar in Kashmir, India, or any of the other famous gardens of the world. There are no thorns on the roses, and the flowers never fade. He may show you the trees that are blooming in the heavenlies.

He may take you to the music room of Heaven. When I saw that room, it was much like the great libraries with high stacks and movable ladders on rails to reach them. I saw angels pulling out manuscripts and dropping them into the mouths of believers who wanted to sing a new song unto the Lord. You may see an angel setting down some new songs and getting ready to impart them to you.

He may show you all the beauties He has prepared for those who love Him.

He may take you into the command room of Heaven and show you how He is ordering the movement of His angels at that moment. You might see the heavenly hosts being sent forth. You might see Him sending and commissioning particular angels to help in particular areas of the world.

God has shown me so many wonderful things about Heaven. One of the things that impresses me most about that heavenly realm is that there are no barriers, no limitations. In the natural, you can't go very far until you find some type of barrier. But when you get in the Spirit and you are in the heavenlies, there are no barriers, no limitations. There are millions of miles open on every side of you.

Many have shared with us their experiences of Heaven. My uncle, Dr. William A. Ward, had marvelous experiences in Heaven, and he told us about them. He was lifted up again and again into the heavenlies. God wants all of us to be anointed to see.

> *Eye hath not seen, nor ear heard, neither have entered into the heart of man, the things which God hath prepared for them that love him.*
> 1 Corinthians 2:9

But that's not the end of the thought.

> *But God hath revealed them unto us by his Spirit.* Verse 10

God wants us to live in the realm of revelation. And we can only live in that realm of revelation as we live in the glory of the Lord.

> *And the glory of the Lord shall be revealed, and all flesh shall see it together: for the mouth of the Lord hath spoken it.* Isaiah 40:5

The time is coming when all flesh together shall see the revelation of the glory of God. In these days God is coming to us individually to show forth His glory, His power, Himself.

We have experienced periods of several weeks at a time in Jerusalem when people were seeing the Lord, not only in visions, but personally. He was coming to them in physical form. They were seeing Him walk the streets of Jerusalem. He was speaking to them. We have had many glorious angelic visitations in which people sat beside angels and talked with them. They stood with angels and were ministered to by them. They could talk by the hour about those experiences. It happens in the glory.

You might say, "Sister Ruth, I'm not spiritual enough for all that yet. I'm a new believer." We often find that new believers come into these things more easily because they don't have anything to *unlearn*. Many have the impression that these things are for a select few. I, myself, was willing to live and travel for years hearing the voice of God and not seeing vision. But since God awakened me to the fact that I needed to see as well as hear, my life has known a fullness that I didn't experience before.

In the natural, I don't know of anything worse than blindness — not being able to see the beauties of nature. For a Christian not to see the Lord, and just walk blindly, is just as bad. Seeing is one of the ways God speaks to us.

We don't need to walk blindly. God's glory is revealed. If we can have faith to believe for people to be healed, if we can have faith for finances, if we can have faith to go to the nations, can't we have faith in the area of worship and believe to see the glory of God? Did not the Lord say, *"If thou wouldest believe, thou shouldest see the glory of the God"* (John 11:40)? God wants us to be anointed in this way, to have that desire in our hearts to see the glory of God realized.

In our campmeetings throughout the years, we have had glorious angelic visitations. We have had experiences in the night in which the glory of God has come and ministered unto the people. The King of Glory is present, as God promised. But in these last days we will see an increase in both His presence and that of His heavenly hosts.

When you lift up your heads in praise and are lifted up by the Spirit into worship, the King of Glory will come in. He will fight your battles for you. He will bring an ease to your ministry and to your personal life. His angels will be increasingly seen, the armies of God present in our services, until the coming of the Lord. The glory of the Lord shall be revealed, and all flesh shall see it together.

If you want to be an effectual intercessor, you must

know the realm of glory. Otherwise, you will live in the realm of man's understanding and spend most of your time praying about all the wrong things. When you move into the realm of the Spirit, He shows you what to target.

For a period of time, a diplomat from the Australian Embassy in Tel Aviv came up to Jerusalem every weekend to attend our services. This was just at the time when China was beginning to open and when there was much activity in the Middle East. He had access to diplomatic pouches, to intelligence information from the Mossad (the Israeli intelligence service), from the CIA, from British Intelligence, from Australia, and from other Western countries. It was his job to send back to the foreign office in Canberra telexes concerning new information and new movements. He told us that the information coming forth in the Spirit in our prayer meetings concerning China was six months ahead of the diplomatic pouches.

One day, while we were in prayer, God showed us that Syria would enter the war in Lebanon. Until that time, she was not actively involved and had kept herself in her own territory.

This man was very excited about what the Lord was showing us and wanted to act on it. He couldn't send a telex, however, saying, "I was in a prayer meeting on Mount Zion and God showed us a vision and we know that Syria is going to enter the war." He needed something more concrete. He searched the local news carefully for any substantiation of this.

Within a day or two, Prime Minister Menachem Begin made a comment that Syria would be entering the war soon. Armed with that new information, the diplomat went to his ambassador saying, "I think we ought to send this information to Canberra."

"That was just an offhand statement," the ambassador answered him. "We can't build something on a passing statement." (Of course, I knew that Menachem Begin never made an offhand statement.)

When our friend tried to press the issue, the ambassador replied, "Listen, I'm having dinner tonight with several of the ambassadors. Let me put out some feelers first. We can always send your message tomorrow."

When he came into the office the next morning, he said, "Send it!" Within a few days, Syria entered the war.

Numerous times there were similar situations in which the Holy Ghost was so very faithful. God wants our praise and worship to bring us into glory and the realm of revelation, so that we can be effective in prayer.

Just before a period of difficult financial times came to Dallas, I was introduced to a well-to-do couple who were believers. As I sat across from them at the Dallas/Fort Worth Airport, sharing a refreshment before departure time, I began to see a ball of red yarn tangled in knots. I couldn't tell the end from the beginning. I knew instantly that the tangled ball represented their finances. I began to describe the vision.

"I am seeing a tangled ball of red yarn, and God is showing me that it is your financial situation. Your finances are so tangled that you can't find the end or the beginning."

"I am seeing the hand of God reach in, take hold of the end, and straighten it all out."

That's all I said, but tears filled their eyes. In just a couple of minutes God had ministered to the need in their life. It came so easily.

While I was in Houston, a friend gave a luncheon party to introduce me to her friends. When I got my plate and sat down, the people nearby were talking about Texas beef. Yet, no sooner had I sat down than I began to see a vision of the lady beside me. I saw three or four arrows going into her heart on either side. I began to describe to her what I was seeing.

I saw the hand of the Lord reaching in to pull out one arrow after another. In just a moment's time, every one of those arrows had been taken out right in front of my eyes.

Just as quickly as I described the vision to her, God

did the work. Tears streamed down her cheeks. It was so easy.

I was leaving China once and intended to fly directly to Jerusalem. The Lord spoke to me and said, "I want you to go to Japan. You don't have time to minister there, but I am going to send you to someone who will be speaking in many conventions. I want you to tell him on what to speak."

"Who are You sending me to?" I asked the Lord.

He reminded me that two years before, Susan and I had spent a little time at Prayer Mountain in Korea with Sister Choi. She didn't speak English, and we didn't speak Korean. She did speak Japanese, however, as do many Koreans (because of the former Japanese occupation). A Japanese brother was there visiting, so she spoke to him and he interpreted her words to us in English.

The only thing I could remember about that Japanese brother was him telling us that he had just built a church between Narita Airport and Tokyo. (That's like saying that he had just built a church between Los Angeles and San Diego.) Now, when the Lord was telling me to go see this man, I had no way of learning anything more about him.

I flew into Tokyo, went directly to one of the airport hotels, got the telephone, and began calling churches in the area. I first called the Baptists. I told them who I was, that I was from Jerusalem, and that

I had met a Japanese man in Korea who had built a church within the past several years that was probably Pentecostal or Charismatic and was located somewhere between Narita Airport and Tokyo. They couldn't help me, but they gave me the number of the Assembly of God church.

I called the Assembly of God church. They didn't know the brother I was looking for or anything about his church, but they did know a brother who moves in Charismatic circles. They gave me his number.

I called the brother and went through the same introduction a third time.

"Sister Ruth," he answered, "I have never met you, but some of our people went to Jerusalem and attended your Bible school. I know the brother you are talking about. Let me give you his telephone number."

When our conversation ended, I called the number he gave me. "Brother," I said, "you probably don't remember me. Two of us, sisters from Jerusalem, met you at Sister Choi's place at Prayer Mountain several years ago."

"Oh, yes, I remember you two sisters from Jerusalem," he answered. "I have often prayed for you. Where are you now?"

"Well, I'm at the airport," I told him. "I have a

message from the Lord for you. I came to Japan just to see you."

"Sister, I am so sorry," he said, "I'm just getting ready to leave for a conference."

"I know," I told him.

"You know?" he asked. "Well, I am packing now and I will leave later today. Could you come quickly?" He gave me instructions for the train.

When I was still on the plane from Hong Kong, I had asked the Lord, "What is the message that this man should preach to the conference?" He reminded me that one day before I left Jerusalem I was praying and He had said to me, *"Kabuki."*

Kabuki, I knew, was a Japanese art form, a traditional play. But when God said *kabuki* to me, I didn't think He was talking about plays. What could He mean?

We had a Japanese brother in our Jerusalem fellowship at that time, and I thought, "When I have time, I must remember to ask the brother what *kabuki* means." But I forgot to do it.

Now, on the plane from Hong Kong to Tokyo, when I asked the Lord what the message was, He said to me again, *"Kabuki."*

I called the Japanese flight attendant over and asked her, "What does the word *kabuki* mean?"

"It's a classical Japanese play," she said.

"Yes," I said, "I know it's a classical Japanese play. But what does the word *kabuki* mean?"

She thought a moment, then replied, "*Ka* means 'song,' *bu* means 'dance,' and *ki* means 'art.' "

I understood immediately that God was speaking about the song/dance art of praising Him.

When I arrived at the train station, the brother met me and took me back to the church where he and his wife lived in some adjoining rooms. We made small talk about my trip to China and about Israel as we drank Japanese tea.

When we finished drinking the tea, he was ready to get down to business. He asked, "Sister, why have you come?"

"I have come," I told him, "to give you the message you are to speak on at the conferences."

He seemed surprised when I said "conferences."

"This is the first conference I have been invited to speak at," he told me. "But I have already been invited to others. What is the message?"

"The answer for revival in Japan," I told him, "can be found in one Japanese word — *kabuki*."

He looked at me strangely, possibly thinking of the Japanese play.

I repeated the word syllable by syllable: "*Ka - bu - ki* — the song/dance art of praising the Lord." Tears filled his eyes.

"I have been praying for the message for the conference," he said. "Each time I prayed, God told me to speak on singing and dancing. I told the Lord that I knew singing would play a very important part in the revival in Japan, but not that ungodly dancing. Each time I prayed I got the same answer, and each time I rejected it."

God had taken me all the way from Jerusalem via China to tell him that revival in Japan would come through singing and dancing.

I ministered to him prophetically. He took me back to the train station. I went back to the airport hotel, got my bags, and boarded the next flight for Jerusalem.

The spirit of revelation works in the midst of the glory revealed. That glory reveals to us that which eye hath not seen nor ear heard.

> *But we speak the wisdom of God in a mystery,*
> *even the hidden wisdom, which God ordained*
> *before the world unto our glory.*
> 1 Corinthians 2:7

There is a certain wisdom that God has ordained unto our glory. Paul said we speak that wisdom. Often we are hoping to speak it. We want to speak it. But Paul said we are already doing it. He said we are speaking the wisdom of God in a mystery. We are speaking even the hidden wisdom which God hath ordained from the foundations of the world unto our glory.

> *For he that speaketh in an unknown tongue speaketh not unto men, but unto God: for no man understandeth him; howbeit in the spirit he speaketh mysteries.*   1 Corinthians 14:2

So, what are we doing every time we pray in tongues? We're speaking mysteries. We're speaking the wisdom of God. Those words you thought were so insignificant are, in reality, a profound mystery in God. Even if you haven't made your first million yet, you can speak the mysteries of God. Yes! You can! We speak the wisdom of God in a mystery. This has been ordained unto our glory.

When we speak in other tongues, we are speaking mysteries. *"No man understandeth us."* Many times people have used this second verse as a criticism of speaking in tongues. The apostle Paul is not using it negatively. He is saying that this is a plus. He is saying, in essence, "Thank God nobody understands. Thank God your understanding is unfruitful. Thank God that you're not just living in the realm of your logic. You're moving over into the spirit man. The spirit is speaking. The spirit is praying. The spirit is understanding."

The eye hasn't seen it. The ear hasn't heard it. The

heart of man has not yet perceived what God has planned. But He reveals it by His Spirit.

We are moving, then, into the revelation of God. God reveals it unto us by His Spirit. What is revealed unto us? What the eye has not seen. What is revealed unto us? What the ear has not heard. What is revealed unto us? What the heart of man has not yet perceived. God causes us to know by revelation the same mysteries that we were speaking in a language we didn't know. And in the midst of those words was hidden wisdom. Suddenly we find that we begin to speak forth that wisdom, because the revelation begins to come forth in our lives.

If you want to live in the realm of supernatural revelation, pray in tongues a lot. Sing in tongues a lot. You are feeding the well. You are singing to the well that will bring forth that release of information. You will flow in revelation knowledge. It might not happen right at the moment, because you don't need it right at the moment. When you do get into a situation where you need it, it will be there.

When I went to Hong Kong to serve the Lord as a young girl, I worked with a group of wealthy men in the Full Gospel Business Men's Fellowship there. About fifty of them were millionaires. Often, one or the other of them would call me with business questions. What did I know? I was eighteen years old and didn't have more than fifty dollars a month to manage. I had no business experience. But God had promised me that if I would seek His face, He would be my wisdom.

Time and again I would sit back and listen to the answers God gave me and be amazed, as if someone else were answering through me. It was my voice that I heard. It was my mouth that was being used. But the words were words of revelation. I had done a lot of praying in tongues. So, when I needed revelation knowledge, that revelation knowledge was there.

God will give it to you too. His revelation knowledge can be applied, not only in the realm of spiritual things, but in the realm of natural things as well.

We reach this revelatory realm through prayer in the Spirit. None of us do it enough. I don't pray enough in the Spirit. Periodically, I like to teach on prayer in the Spirit, because I get stirred myself and find myself waking up in the night, praying in tongues.

If you want to live in the realm of revelation knowledge, then you need to speak the wisdom of God in a mystery. God has revealed the mystery unto us by His Spirit. Those who speak it first in a mystery come to understand it. Why? Because *"the Spirit searcheth all things, yea, the deep things of God."*

There are things that we would all love to know about God. But we wouldn't have any idea in which book we should look them up or in which part of the Bible we should search them out. Our concordances and other study helps are not able to bring into focus the things we sometimes have in our spirits that we want God to answer. But, thank the Lord, we have the Holy Ghost who is the Researcher.

A college professor, when writing a treatise, has researchers who do all the background work and lay out the material. Then he, as the author, just puts it all together in a meaningful way. We have the Holy Ghost. He is searching out the deep and hidden truths. He is better than the most powerful computer available.

God gives supernatural, revelatory knowledge to those who are seeking Him, praying in the Spirit, letting revelation come. We speak the wisdom of God in a mystery. *"The Spirit searcheth all things, yea, the deep things of God."*

> *For what man knoweth the things of a man, save the spirit of man which is in him? even so the things of God knoweth no man, but the Spirit of God.*
> *Now we have received, not the spirit of the world, but the spirit which is of God; that we might know the things that are freely given to us of God.*   1 Corinthians 2:11-12

I want to encourage you to pray in the Spirit and sing in the Spirit more than you ever have. I preached in a Methodist church in North Carolina. I encouraged a visiting pastor over and over to pray in tongues. He said, "I have spoken in tongues more this week than I have during the ten years since I received this experience."

God not only gives it to us as a gift. He gives it to make us effective in the Kingdom of God. We need to be those praying in the Spirit, singing in the Spirit. We can praise in tongues. We can worship in tongues. We can stand in the glory in tongues. If we do, the revelation comes.

I know that singing in the Spirit will be a great part of the coming revival. There will be whole services in which congregations will stand in the glory and worship in the Spirit.

From the day that God spoke this to me, I have sung in the Spirit every day. I have many friends who sing in the Spirit very beautifully. Their songs sound almost heavenly. At first I was hesitant to sing in the Spirit, because my singing was not as beautiful as theirs. I purposed anyway to sing in the Spirit every day until my ability to yield to the Holy Spirit in that way became greater. When God reveals a spiritual truth to us, we have to flow in it — even in an elementary way — until maturity comes to us in that gifting. (The gift does not mature, but our ability to yield to the Spirit and flow in it does.)

I wasn't visionary. Others were having visions and revelations, and I was always thrilled to hear what God was showing them. I heard the voice of the Lord clearly, but didn't personally receive visions. Part of the reason was that we were not taught to believe for it. We must exercise faith in worship. We exercise it for salvation, for healing, for the baptism of the Holy Spirit, and for financial miracles. But we are seldom taught to exercise our faith in worship. Let us use our faith to move into the glory realm so that we can see and know.

My other problem was that I had never asked to see. When I started asking, I started seeing. One of the reasons I hadn't asked before was my misunderstanding of what Jesus said to Thomas.

> *Jesus saith unto him, Thomas, because thou hast seen me, thou hast believed: blessed are they that have not seen, and yet have believed.*
>
> John 20:29

I accepted the fact that it was fine if I didn't see. Many years later, when God began to challenge me to see, He let me know that this verse had nothing to do with my seeing in the realm of the Spirit.

What God is doing today is not brand-new, but

He is doing it for more people. We used to be content to have one or two people be blessed in a particular service. We went home rejoicing that Sister Jones got a blessing. Now, God is doing a new thing. He wants us all to have the same experiences. In the natural, we can all sit down in front of a television, turn to the same channel, and watch the same program. In the glory realm, we can all have a corporate vision. We can have a corporate revelation. We can all see and know and perceive by the Spirit of God. Let the glory lift you into the realm of revelation.

The case of Thomas was different. He was trying to get the Lord to prove something to him. Ask for visions and you will receive visions.

Susan, who was an Episcopalian, started having visions from the moment she was filled with the Spirit. God taught her the Bible by vision. One day she said to me, "Ruth, you do see vision."

"Oh, no, I don't," I answered. "I don't see vision." (Some people are almost proud that they don't: "Other people need those things. I don't need aids or signs to help me hear from God.")

"Oh, no! I don't see any visions," I asserted.

"Yes! You do see visions," she insisted.

"No, I don't," I continued stubbornly.

"Why is it, then," she asked, "that when you prophesy, I hear you say, 'I see so and so'?"

I had to think about that for a moment. I know I don't lie, and I certainly wouldn't be lying while I was prophesying — if I did lie. "Well," I answered, "I see, but I don't see."

We spend so much time explaining away something God has already given to us. "I see, but I don't see."

From that day on, I began to take notice of what was happening while I prophesied, and I learned that she was correct. Although the vision was not the most important thing, God was giving me help as I was prophesying over these people. The vision was revealing to me what I was to say. Vision is one of the important ways God speaks to us.

> *I will stand upon my watch, and set me upon the tower, and will watch to see what he will say unto me.*
> *And the Lord answered me, and said, Write the vision, and make it plain upon tables, that he may run that readeth it.* Habakkuk 2:1-2

The glory brings revelation!

The Glory Brings a Knowing

Hosanna

Words and Music by Ruth Heflin

He answered and said unto them, Because it is given unto you to know the mysteries of the kingdom of heaven, but to them it is not given. For whosoever hath, to him shall be given, and he shall have more abundance: but whosoever hath not, from him shall be taken away even that he hath.

Therefore speak I to them in parables: because they seeing see not; and hearing they hear not, neither do they understand.

And in them is fulfilled the prophecy of Esaias, which saith, By hearing ye shall hear, and shall not understand; and seeing ye shall see, and shall not perceive:

For this people's heart is waxed gross, and their ears are dull of hearing, and their eyes they have closed; lest at any time they should see with their eyes, and hear with their ears, and should understand with their heart, and should be converted, and I should heal them.

But blessed are your eyes, for they see: and your ears, for they hear.

For verily I say unto you, That many prophets and righteous men have desired to see those things which ye see, and have not seen them; and to hear those things which ye hear, and have not heard them.

Jesus

"It is given unto you to know." There is a gift of the Lord, the gift of knowing, knowing by the Spirit, knowing by the seeing of the spiritual eye, know-

ing by the hearing of the spiritual ear. This is a gifting of God which operates in the glory.

God wants us to be those who know the mysteries of the Kingdom. He wants revelation knowledge to be in our spirits. It hasn't all been revealed yet. Revelation is still working, and God wants to put revelation knowledge and understanding into your spirit, as well. He is directing our eyesight upward into the heavenlies. He wants us not to be so caught up with those things round about us, but to be caught up with those things that are above, in the eternal world.

I don't find enough people who are eager to learn the things of the Spirit. We were blessed because my grandmother was a great Bible scholar, not only from the intellectual standpoint, but also spiritually, because of her hunger for the Word. She searched things out. She wrote to men who were considered to be great scholars of the Word and posed to them some of her most difficult questions. These were not ordinary Bible questions, but things of the deeper riches of the Word of God. She searched for those truths as a miner would for a rare diamond or a vein of gold. The Scripture says that God's Word is more to be desired than gold (Psalm 19:10).

Grandmother wrote to Dr. Evans and to several other great men, asking them what they thought on a number of issues. They wrote back and said, "Sister Ward, we haven't thought of the answer yet. In fact, we hadn't even thought of the question until you posed it."

It's good for us to have questions, but not from the standpoint of being critical, or doubtful. (Some people are always questioning everything. They have a questioning mentality and never come to an understanding of the answer.) Having questions shows that we are searching after God. We want to know more. We wonder about things. We wonder who might have the revelation.

On numerous occasions the Lord has sent me to great men of God to instruct them a little more on something they were seeking Him about. He sent me to show them the truth from an angle they hadn't looked at before. In other realms, they were way beyond me. But in an area where God had led me, I was able to give them some assistance. We don't always have the luxury of sitting down with someone who understands us and talking intelligently about the things that trouble us.

When I was fifteen I had a wonderful experience. Mother was preaching in Callao, Virginia, several times a week, and since she didn't drive in those days, I would drive her there. All the way down and all the way back I could ask her questions and listen intently to her responses. She was gracious to answer every question, although I am sure it tired her.

Sometime that next year, I was driving one night while we were returning home from a convention in Atlanta, Georgia. In the middle of the night I was conscious that I had taken a wrong turn somewhere. Mother was nodding in the front seat. I said, "Mother, would you look and see what route we are supposed to be on. Is it 544?"

"Oh, Honey," she answered wearily, "I'm so tired. Wait until tomorrow and we'll discuss what Matthew 5:44 means."

"Mother," I said, "I wasn't asking you about the Bible. I was asking you about the road."

The incident became a family joke.

I have been blessed to have spiritual people to turn to. But later, during many years of my life, I traveled among people who did not speak my language. In conventions of ten thousand people, in India, sometimes only one person spoke English. Because he was my interpreter, when he wasn't translating for me or preaching himself, he was usually doing administrative work. Most of the time I traveled alone across India and across other countries on buses, on boats, on trains, and on planes. During those periods, I began to develop with the Lord that same relationship I had developed with my mother. "Lord, what about this? What about that?"

God wants us to tap into the riches of His Kingdom. He doesn't want us to remain as babes.

When Susan received all those early visions about the Bible, it was because, night after night, she stayed on her knees at the altar for hours at a time. When she told me what she had seen, I knew she had never read about those things. I would tell her where to find them in the Bible so that she could read them for herself and see how God was teaching her — by the Spirit.

Most of us, when we fall out under the power of God (or "rest in the Spirit," as some say), get up too quickly. God wants us to stay there. He doesn't put us on the floor just to show us He can do it. That's His operating table. At times we are not even conscious. But, whether you are conscious or not, let vision flow. Let God show you things.

"But what if that's not happening?" I can hear someone asking. Well, just stay there and praise and worship and adore. God will be putting things into your spirit without your even realizing it. Then, when you stand to minister, you will stand in greater authority, and teachings will come forth from your mouth that you will wonder where you have learned. Know that God placed them in the depths of your soul, put them into your understanding, put them into your spirit — while you were out under the power.

We must linger more at His altar and let Him cause us to know. It is given unto us to know.

> *In a dream, in a vision of the night, when deep*
> *sleep falleth upon men, in slumberings upon*
> *the bed;*
> *Then he openeth the ears of men, and sealeth*
> *their instruction.* Job 33:15-16

If believers would have one outstanding characteristic, it should be confidence that they have a knowing in their lives. Believers should be growing in confidence. Those who possess a knowing are immovable, unshakable.

It is the nature of the believer to know. It is given unto you to know, not just to know the ABC's, but to know the mysteries of the Kingdom of God.

When we speak it forth, the mystery does not remain a mystery. God begins to bring it to the light, so that we have a knowledge and an understanding of those things that we have spoken in tongues, in the Spirit.

> *The secret things belong unto the LORD our*
> *God: but those thing which are revealed belong*
> *unto us and to our children for ever, that we*
> *may do all the words of this law.*
> Deuteronomy 29:29

Will you immediately interpret what you said? No. You may pray for hours in tongues. Then, when you get up to speak, that revelation might come in two or three sentences. But it will be such a powerful revelation that it will feed multitudes. We must feed the people with manna from above, and that manna from above is revelation knowledge. God wants us to feed it to the nations of the world. He doesn't give you just enough for your household. He gives you enough for the household of faith, for the Body of Christ universal.

When I was a young girl, the Lord said to me, "Desire not earthly knowledge or earthly wisdom. If you will seek My face, I will give you My knowledge and My wisdom." Later, He demonstrated to me His faithfulness in giving me wisdom and knowledge.

My good friend Mrs. Bruce Crane Fisher owns Westover on the James River, the finest example of Georgian architecture in America. People come from all over the world to Virginia to see it. One day, when I was traveling overseas, I was suddenly conscious that there were things about her that I didn't know that I wanted to know. We had been friends for a number of years. We had prayed together and we had had good times together. Yet I had always been so busy, rushing in and out of Virginia, that there were things about her that I didn't know.

I decided that the first thing I would do when I got back to America would be to call her and arrange a time to visit with her.

"Why don't you come down for lunch tomorrow?" she said.

I went without telling her what was on my mind. We had a nice visit. I discovered, for the first time, that she had been raised in Prague, Czechoslovakia. Her grandfather had been the United States ambassador to Peking during the Wilson administration, and her father was the American ambassador to Czechoslovakia when she was a child. Her uncle, Mr. Charles Crane, was advisor to King Ibn Saud. As we talked longer, we eventually spoke about more personal things. I learned so much about my friend.

It takes time to get to know someone. Also, you must want to know. Sometimes we say to the Lord, "Anything You want me to know, just tell me."

He is longing for someone who loves Him enough to say, "Lord, I want to see what the skirt of Your garment looks like. Would You show me, Lord? May I see Your eyes more clearly? Lord, would You tell me something? Would You tell me what You think about China at the moment?"

I always laugh when Mother tells about asking the Lord when it is that the former and latter rain will come in the same month. She said to the Lord, "If You could tell 'little old me' ..."

He is saying to us, "I thought you would never ask. I have so many things that I want to tell you, that I've been wanting to share with you, that I desire to reveal to you. But you were so indifferent to My presence.

"You were like those who are in a hurry to get to McDonald's drive-in window to get a quick hamburger. You didn't have time to sit down and enjoy the atmosphere. You didn't want to enjoy the music. You didn't want to enjoy the decor. You didn't want to feel the ambiance of the place. You just wanted to get in and out quickly.

"I want you to sit down with Me in My Kingdom. I want to reveal many things to you. I want you to sit down with Me at My throne. *It is given unto you to know.*"

"But to them it is not given." Why? Because their hearts were not sincerely seeking after the things of God. They just wanted knowledge for the sake of knowledge. They wanted knowledge for the sake of argument. They wanted knowledge for the sake of discourse. They wanted knowledge so that people would recognize them as great orators. They didn't really want to know.

Some want to know. I want to know. I want to know Him. I want to know those things pertaining to Him. I want to know those things pertaining to His kingdom. I want to know His mysteries.

A mystery is just a hidden thing, a secret. I want to know the secret things, the intimate things of God.

They are concealed, but He wants to reveal them, and I want to know them.

If you have the same desire, give Him a little more time. Sit down more with Him. Ask Him questions like the prophets did:

"Lord, what meaneth this?"

"What meaneth that?"

"Lord, what about this?"

He delights in showing us the answers — by His Spirit.

> *But blessed are your eyes, for they see: and your ears, for they hear.*
> *For verily I say unto you, That many prophets and righteous men have desired to see those things which ye see, and have not seen them; and to hear those things which ye hear, and have not heard them.*   Matthew 13:16-17

You are blessed! You are blessed to see and hear. And God wants you to see and hear more in the days to come. Enter into the glory through praise and worship and receive the knowing of the Spirit.

The glory brings a knowing!

The Glory Brings Perspective

No Limitations

Words and Music by Ruth Heflin

No lim....i.......ta...tions in the Spir.........................it.

No lim...i.......ta...tions in the glo...........................ry.

No lim.....i.......ta...tions in the Spir.........................it.

No lim...i.......ta..tions in the glo...........................ry.

And the nations of them which are saved shall walk in the light of it: and the kings of the earth do bring their glory and honour into it.

John

The revelation of God begins with the face of Jesus and continues with the glories of Heaven, but it always finishes on the Earth. Until Jesus comes, His one concern is this Earth. The difference is that when He shows you the Earth, you will see it from Heaven's point of view, from His perspective. When you see the Earth in that way, its problems are not so overwhelming.

He will show you the concerns of His heart — perhaps a place, or a situation you were unaware of. He lets you glimpse it from eternity's point of view and drops a little understanding into your spirit so that you can pray for and believe for that place or situation.

In the rarefied atmosphere of Tibet, at fifteen thousand feet, you see things differently. It seems that you can see forever. The water looks different. The sky looks different. Everything looks different. When we are standing on the mount of God, everything looks different. We see with different eyes.

God must lift us into the glory realm so that we can see the Earth from Heaven's perspective. We have lived on this earthly level so long that we see things totally out of perspective.

When Jim Irwin went to the moon, the thing that amazed him was that the Earth appeared to be the size of a golf ball. It was life-changing for him. He determined that if God could love this small Earth so much that He was willing to send His Son, then he would go back to Earth and dedicate his life to the ministry. He took a golf ball with him wherever he went as a reminder of that perspective.

The enemy is the magnifier. He magnifies things out of proportion. Even when we don't have big problems, we see the little things magnified. Our prayer lives are guided by Earth's magnification and not by Heaven's viewpoint. So, when we are lifted into the glory, and see the Lord, we always end up with a new perspective of the Earth.

Most people, once they have seen the Lord, feel that it is enough. They are so excited, "Oh, I've seen the Lord! I've seen the Lord!" But He wants to show us more. The fuller vision should show us something of the Earth. We need to see this Earth from Heaven's perspective.

If we're not careful, we pick up the newspaper, read about a certain problem, and start praying about that problem. Sometimes that problem takes up all our prayer time. Maybe God wanted us to pray about some need that was not mentioned in the newspaper or on television. He wants people whom He can lift up in the Spirit and cause them to focus in on a particular need somewhere in the world. We can be effective in prayer when we have seen the need from Heaven's standpoint.

Recently, I had an experience in the Spirit in which the head of an eagle came down over my head almost like a mask at a masquerade party. Then, the calf's head came down over mine. As I searched the Scriptures I found that the eagle's head and the calf's head are on the same side of the living creatures. The eagle represents the visionary, revelatory aspect, whereas the calf represents the servanthood of the Body of Christ.

When people consume vision only upon themselves, there can be a tendency for it to become unbalanced. When vision and revelation are linked with service to the Body of Christ, they stay in proper relationship to the whole.

Get Heaven's perspective.

For if I pray in an unknown tongue, my spirit
prayeth, but my understanding is unfruitful.
What is it then? I will pray with the spirit, and
I will pray with the understanding also: I will
sing with the spirit, and I will sing with the
understanding also.

1 Corinthians 14:14-15

I want you to see God's priorities. Usually we do the reverse. We pray with the understanding and "also" with the Spirit. Most of the time we pray in English or whatever our natural tongue is. Then, we "also" pray a little in other tongues. But the emphasis of the Holy Ghost is *"I will pray in the Spirit and I will also pray in the understanding. I will sing in the Spirit and I will also sing with the understanding."* The more you get in the Spirit, the more you're going to be speaking and singing and praising and worshiping in other tongues — by the Spirit of the living God.

Let the glory change your priorities. Get God's perspective. See as He sees. We are going to see such revival on the Earth that whole nations will come into the Kingdom of God.

And the city had no need of the sun, neither of
the moon, to shine in it: for the glory of God
did lighten it, and the Lamb is the light thereof.

*And the nations of them which are saved shall
walk in the light of it: and the kings of the earth
do bring their glory and honour into it.*
Revelation 21:23-24

Saved nations? Some of you can hardly believe
for your own spouses to get saved. Get into the
heavenlies, and not only will you believe for your
spouses, you'll believe for the nations. If you stay in
the earthly realm, you will have a problem believing just for the person next door. But if you get in
the Spirit, you can believe for continents.

The Word of God says there will be saved nations.
We are going to see great revival. Israel will be one
of the saved nations. I know, because the apostle
Paul prophesied, *"All Israel shall be saved"* (Romans
11:26).

But Israel will not be the only saved nation. *"The
nations of them which are saved ..."* In that realm of
glory, your faith is released to believe for the greater
things that God has. You begin to know the King of
Glory. You know that He's the One who fights the
battles. He's the One who's bringing the victories.

When I was a young person in Hong Kong, I already had a vision for the nations. Some of my
companions didn't understand that. They wondered
why I wasn't satisfied with just Hong Kong.

They asked me, "When did this concept of the nations first come into your spirit?" I don't know. But I was raised in the glory, and when God is speaking, He always speaks the fullness of the vision. His vision is always the whole world. When you hear God talk a lot, you begin to get God's ideas in your spirit and begin to be conscious of what He is thinking.

His desires are toward the nations. I seldom say, "Jerusalem," without including "Israel, and the nations." God's desire for Jerusalem and for all Israel is that through Jerusalem and Israel the ends of the Earth be blessed and saved.

The glory brings perspective!

Praise ... until the
spirit of
worship
comes.

Worship ... until the
glory comes.

Then ...

Stand in the glory!

Postscript

The Heavens Are Open

Words and Music by Ruth Heflin

The heavens are o.....................pen................... , and I...... see Je.....................sus..................... . The heavens are o..........................pen................... , and I see the Lord................ .... The heavens are o..... ....pen................... ... , and I....... see Je.....................sus..................... . The heavens are o.........................pen................... , And I see the Lord... .

2. Sing hallelujah! Sing hallelujah!
   The heavens are open, and I see the Lord.
   Sing hallelujah! Sing hallelujah!
   The heavens are open, and I see the Lord.

I will proceed to do a marvellous work among this people, even a marvellous work and a wonder.

Isaiah

I am so thrilled that God is using my book *Glory* to help bring in the last-day revival. Some have said that God was already speaking to them concerning many of the things mentioned in the book, but they didn't have anyone to confirm these things to them, and they didn't have enough confidence to act on them on their own. When they read them in my book, they were so glad to know that others were hearing the same things from God.

One sister in Invercargill, New Zealand, said that her church had been touched by revival for about two years, but they didn't know how to go on from there. When she read *Glory*, she knew this was the answer.

After reading *Glory*, many pastors flew to Jerusalem to be in our meetings, and they took home, as presents, enough *Glory* books for their staffs. The wonderful letters that I have received of lives and ministries changed by reading *Glory* would fill another book.

One February, I met Marge Lottis of Salem, Oregon, at the evening dinner meeting of the annual Presidential Prayer Breakfast in Washington, D.C. I gave her a copy of my book, and a week or two later she telephoned me at the campmeeting in Virginia where I was speaking. She said that reading my book had been life-changing for her. The day before, floodwaters had risen in the river in front of her house. She gathered intercessors together and told them that they were going to try a new way of interceding she had just read about. The group praised the Lord and danced before Him in front of the window overlooking the rising river. Some of the people from the news media who were on the bank of the river looked up, and seeing these people at the window waving their hands, thought they were waving at them, and waved back.

While the little group was praising God, the river stopped rising. One of them was moved to declare that the river should turn and flow in the direction of the agricultural land which needed the water, and not in the direction of their houses. Later, they all watched as the miracle took place. The river turned and watered the farmlands, and their houses were spared. This miracle occurred as they praised and worshiped the Lord.

Later, Marge shared truths from *Glory* at a meeting in Montana. Tears streamed down the cheeks of grown men who were hearing these truths for the first time. Their souls, which were so hungry for God, were beginning to be as a "watered garden."

Friends are passing *Glory* to other friends. A senator received a copy from a sister who wanted to bless him. After reading it, he telephoned to say he had been looking for this for ten years.

I am indebted to many people for making it all possible. Katherine Fujino of Honolulu, Hawaii, helped to finance the publishing of the second printing. Margaret McWatters of Atlanta, Georgia, bought boxes of the book and gave them away, sowing them into the lives of ministers, as well as lay people. Ione Lathrop made it possible for me to sow *Glory* into the lives of people and churches all over the world.

The Brownsville Assembly of God of Pensacola, Florida, the church that has been experiencing revival fires since Father's Day of 1995, made my book available to people coming to the revival from all over the United States and also from abroad.

Glory has now been translated and printed in more than a dozen languages, and more manuscripts are ready for printing in other languages. If you would like to translate it into a language in which it is not already translated, please inform me. We printed ten thousand copies of *Glory* in Russian and distributed them freely to the churches across Russia. As I was writing this postscript, three Russian pastors were visiting us in Jerusalem. They read *Glory* in Russian and were greatly enlarged.

If you have read *Glory* and have been blessed, please read it again. I always encourage everyone to read it three times, because with each reading there is a birthing of new understanding and experience.

May God bless and enlarge you in the reading.

Ruth Heflin

Other Worship Songs

by

Ruth Ward Heflin

224

Jerusalem, a House of Prayer
Words and Music by Ruth Heflin

Continued:

Verses:

1. A House of Prayer .... for all na........tions.

A House of Prayer .... for all the world.

A House of Prayer..................... , for... all peo..........ple.

Jeru...sa........lem........................... , Jeru....sa.......lem.

2. Prevailing prayer is the answer
   For Jerusalem, for all the world.
   Prevailing prayer is the answer.
   Jerusalem, Jerusalem.

3. Holy is the Lord, in Jerusalem.
   Holy is the Lord, in Jerusalem.
   Holy is the Lord among His people.
   Holy, holy, holy, holy.

I Ask for the Nations

Words and Music by
RUTH WARD HEFLIN

In the name___ of Je-
(May they not___ be) na-

sus,___ In the name of the Lord.___
ked.___ May they not be a - shamed___

I come___ to Thee, oh, God.___ In the
to stand be - fore Thee, oh, Lord___ on that

name   of   the   Lord._____   I   ask   not   for
great   judge-ment   day._____   Oh   may   they   be

rich - es,_____   I   ask   not   for   fame._____
spot - less _____   and   may   they   be   clothed _____

_____   I   ask   for   the   na - tions_____
oh   may   they   know   Je - sus_____

_____   in   Je - sus'   that   day   at   Thy   name._____
throne._____   I

ask for the na - tions, _____ I

call them by name. _____ I pre-

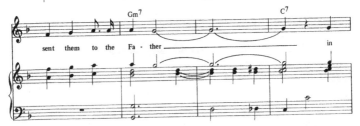

sent them to the Fa - ther _____ in

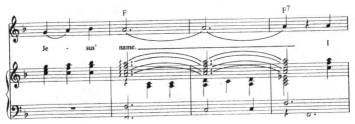

Je - sus' name. _____ I

ask for the na - tions, I

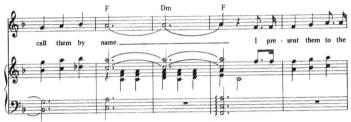

call them by name. I pre - sent them to the

Fa - ther in Je - sus' name.

May they not be

He Gave Me

Words and Music by
RUTH WARD HEFLIN and
SUSAN SHARP WOODAMAN

call. He's my God, and I'm His child, and He loves me._____ Yes, He
door. He's my God, and I'm His child, and He loves me._____
star. He's my God, and I'm His child, and He loves me.

loves me,_____ Tru-ly loves me._____ His de-sire is ev-er toward

me._____ And I love Him,_____ tru-ly love Him._____ My de-

sire is_____ ev-er toward Him.

2. One soul I
3. One land I

Him._____

And So We Wait

Words and Music by
RUTH WARD HEFLIN

1. And so we wait, we wait un-til He comes for us. ___ And so we wait, with joy and ex-pec - ta - tion. ___ And

so we wait, know-ing that each day will be____ prep-a - ra-tion for the

com - ing of the Lord. We wait not as those who

have no hope. We work not as those who re - ceive no re -

ward, we has - ten not as those who run in ____ vain, as we

wait for the com-ing of the Lord. 2. A glimpse of Him

will all our hope and joy ful-fill. A smile from Him will be life's great re-

ward. To be with Him nev-er more to know the pain

of sep-a-ra-tion from the One we've wait-ed for. We

So Many Miracles

Words and Music by Ruth Heflin

The Flutter of Their Wings

Words and Music by
RUTH WARD HEFLIN

Not too slow, with spirit

I can feel the flut-ter, flut-ter, flut-ter of their wings,_____ The liv-ing crea-tures in the wheel as they sing;_____ Ho-ly, Ho-ly, Ho-ly to our God, Which was, and is, and is to come, I can feel the flut-ter, flut-ter, flut-ter of their wings._____ I can feel the flut-ter, flut-ter, flut-ter of their wings,_____ That pro-claim the soon com-ing of our King;_____ As the

an - gels hov-er near, Je - sus Christ will soon ap - pear, I can feel the flut-ter, flut-ter,

flut-ter of their wings. 3. I can feel the flut - ter, flut - ter,

flut-ter of their wings, As they cried Ho - ly, Ho - ly, Ho - ly to our

King; So I fell on my face for the Glo - ry in this

place, Make me feel the flut - ter, flut - ter, flut - ter of their wings.

Why Don't You Let Go And Let God

Words and Music by Ruth Heflin

Copyright © 1988—Ruth Heflin

I Want to Consider You

Words and Music by Ruth Heflin

I want to consider.., to consid...........er.. You. I

want to consider......., to con..sid.................. er You. I

want to consider........, to consid.....................er.. You. I

want to consid...........er You...............................

2. Beyond the moon and stars
   You are, You are.
   Beyond the moon and stars
   You are, You are.
   Beyond the moon and stars
   You are, You are
   I want to consider You.

3. From eternity to eternity
   You are, You are.
   From eternity to eternity
   You are, You are.
   From eterninty to eternity
   You are, You are.
   I want to consider You.

4. Without You there would be
   No need for melody.
   Without You there would be
   No need for melody
   Without You there would be
   No need for melody.
   I want to consider You.

5. Consider the lilies
   How they grow.
   No toiling, no spinning,
   Yet they grow.
   Consider the lilies
   How they grow.
   And you will consider Me.

240

Wheel Within a Wheel

Words and Music by Ruth Heflin

There's a wheel within a wheel, and it's turning in me. It's turn..ing in me. Its turn.....ing in me. There's a wheel...... within a wheel, and it's turn....ing in me. It's turning in the glo...........................ry.............................. .

2. There's a fire within a fire,
And it's burning in me.
It's burning in me.
It's burning in me.
There's a fire within a fire,
And it's burning in me.
It's burning in the glory.

3. I can see. I can see.
I can see the glory.
I can see the glory.
I can see the glory.
I can see. I can see.
I can see the glory.
I can see the glory.

4. You are. You are.
You are my glory.
You are my glory.
You are my glory.
You are. You are.
You are my glory.
You are my glory.